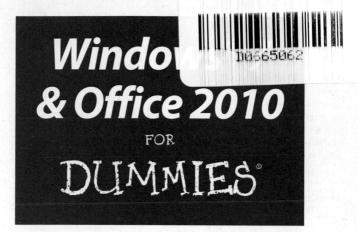

Windows & Office 2010

FOR

DUMMIES

by Andy Rathbone and
Wallace Wang

WILEY

Wiley Publishing, Inc.

Windows® 7 and Office 2010 For Dummies®

Published by
Wiley Publishing, Inc.
111 River Street
Hoboken, NJ 07030-5774

www.wiley.com

Copyright © 2011 by Wiley Publishing, Inc., Indianapolis, Indiana

Published by Wiley Publishing, Inc., Indianapolis, Indiana

Published simultaneously in Canada

For general information on our other products and services, please contact our Customer Care Department within the U.S. at 877-762-2974, outside the U.S. at 317-572-3993, or fax 317-572-4002.

For technical support, please visit www.wiley.com/techsupport.

Wiley also publishes its books in a variety of electronic formats. Some content that appears in print may not be available in electronic books.

Library of Congress Control Number: 2010939501

ISBN: 978-0-470-94188-1

Manufactured in the United States of America

10 9 8 7 6 5 4 3

WILEY

Publisher's Acknowledgments

We're proud of this book; please send us your comments at http://dummies.custhelp.com. For other comments, please contact our Customer Care Department within the U.S. at 877-762-2974, outside the U.S. at 317-572-3993, or fax 317-572-4002.

Some of the people who helped bring this book to market include the following:

Acquisitions and Editorial

Project Editor: Blair J. Pottenger

Executive Editor: Bob Woerner

Editorial Manager: Kevin Kirschner

Media Development Project Manager: Laura Moss-Hollister

Media Development Assistant Project Manager: Jenny Swisher

Editorial Assistant: Amanda Graham

Sr. Editorial Assistant: Cherie Case

Cartoons: Rich Tennant (www.the5thwave.com)

Composition Services

Senior Project Coordinator: Kristie Rees

Layout and Graphics: Kathie Rickard

Proofreaders: Jessica Kramer, Evelyn Wellborn

Indexer: BIM Indexing & Proofreading Services

Special Help: Anne Sullivan, Kathie Richard

Publishing and Editorial for Technology Dummies

    Richard Swadley, Vice President and Executive Group Publisher

    Andy Cummings, Vice President and Publisher

    Mary Bednarek, Executive Acquisitions Director

    Mary C. Corder, Editorial Director

Publishing for Consumer Dummies

    Diane Graves Steele, Vice President and Publisher

Composition Services

    Debbie Stailey, Director of Composition Services

Table of Contents

Introduction

● ●

*W*elcome to *Windows 7 & Office 2010 For Dummies,* your resource for Microsoft's new operating system and office productivity software. You're no dummy, that's for sure. But when it comes to Windows 7 and Office 2010, the fascination just isn't there. You want to get your work done, stop, and move on to something more important.

That's where this book comes in handy. Instead of becoming a Windows 7 and Office 2010 expert, you'll know just enough to get by quickly, cleanly, and with a minimum of pain so that you can move on to the more pleasant things in life.

About This Book

Don't try to read this book in one sitting; there's no need. Instead, treat this book like a dictionary or an encyclopedia. Turn to the page with the information you need and say, "Ah, so that's what they're talking about." Then put down the book and move on.

How This Book Is Organized

The information in this book has been well sifted. This book contains two parts, and each part is divided into chapters relating to the part's theme. Here are the categories (the envelope, please).

Part I: Windows 7

This part introduces you to Windows 7 and dissects its backbone: its opening screen and username buttons, the mammoth Start button menu that fetches all your important stuff, and your computer's desktop — the background where all your programs live. It explains how to move windows around and click the right buttons at the right time.

This part of the book also shows you how to prod programs into action, surf the Internet, customize Windows 7 to your personal needs, and have a little fun playing with media. In a nutshell, this section explains the Windows 7 stuff that everybody thinks that you already know.

Part II: Microsoft Office 2010

To use Microsoft Office 2010, you need to know how to find the commands you need. This part of the book focuses on showing you how to use the Ribbon user interface that appears in all Office 2010 programs. By the time you finish this part of the book, you'll feel comfortable using any program in Office 2010.

This part of the book explains the basics of using Word, Excel, Outlook, PowerPoint, and Access. You become familiar with using Office and read about different techniques you can use to work with Office even faster than before. By the time you finish this part of the book, you'll be much more comfortable using Office 2010.

Part III: The Part of Tens

Everybody loves lists (except during tax time). This part contains lists of ten aggravating things about Windows 7 (and how to fix them) and ten keystroke shortcuts you can use in Office 2010 to increase your productivity.

Icons Used in This Book

Icons highlight important or useful information.

This icon alerts you about juicy information that makes computing easier: a tried-and-true method for keeping the cat from sleeping on top of the monitor, for example.

Don't forget to remember these important points. (Or at least dog-ear the pages so that you can look them up again a few days later.)

The computer won't explode while you're performing the delicate operations associated with this icon. Still, wearing gloves and proceeding with caution is a good idea.

Are you moving to Windows 7 from Windows Vista? This icon alerts you to areas where 7 works significantly differently from its predecessor.

Where to Go from Here

Now, you're ready for action. Give the pages a quick flip and scan a section or two that you know you'll need later. Please remember, this is *your* book — your weapon against the computer nerds who've inflicted this whole complicated computer concept on you. Please circle any paragraphs you find useful, highlight key concepts, add your own sticky notes, and doodle in the margins next to the complicated stuff.

Part I
Windows 7

In this part...

Most people are dragged into Windows 7 without a choice. Their new computers probably came with Windows 7 already installed. Or maybe the office switched to Windows 7, and everyone has to learn it except for the boss, who still doesn't have a computer. Or maybe Microsoft's marketing hype pushed you into it.

Whatever your situation, this part gives a refresher on Windows basics and buzzwords like dragging and dropping, cutting and pasting, and tugging at vanishing toolbars.

This part explains how Windows 7 has changed things for the better and how to navigate and manipulate Windows 7 by poking and prodding its sensitive parts with the mouse.

This part of the book also helps you get some work done. For example, here's where you find out how to locate and work with folders, files, and programs. It also covers how to surf the Web and the things you can do to protect Windows 7. This part ends with some fun stuff by exploring the various Windows 7 media options.

Chapter 1

Introducing Windows 7

In This Chapter

▶ Getting to know Windows 7

▶ Discovering the new features in Windows 7

C hances are good that you've heard about Windows: the boxes and windows and mouse pointer that greet you whenever you turn on your computer. This chapter helps you understand why Windows lives inside your computer and introduces Microsoft's latest Windows version, called *Windows 7.*

What Is Windows 7, and Why Are You Using It?

Created and sold by a company called Microsoft, Windows is an *operating system,* meaning it controls the way you work with your computer. It's been around for more than 20 years, and the latest whiz-bang version is called *Windows 7.*

Windows gets its name from all the cute little windows it places on your monitor. Each window shows information, such as a picture, a program that

you're running, or a baffling technical reprimand.
Windows controls every window and each part of
your computer. When you turn on your computer,
Windows jumps onto the screen and supervises any
running programs.

In addition to controlling your computer and boss-
ing around your programs, Windows 7 comes with
a bunch of free programs. Although your computer
can run without these programs, they're nice to
have. These programs let you do different things,
like write and print letters, browse the Internet, play
music, and store your digital photographs.

And why are you using Windows 7? If you're like
most people, you didn't have much choice. Nearly
every computer sold since October 22, 2009 comes
with Windows 7 preinstalled. Chances are good that
you, your neighbors, your boss, your kids at school,
and millions of other people around the world are
using Windows.

✔ Microsoft took pains (and several years of
work) to make Windows 7 the most secure version of Windows yet.

✔ Windows makes it easy for several people to
share a single computer. Each person receives
his or her own user account. When users click
their name at the Windows opening screen,
they see their *own* work — just the way they
left it.

✔ The powerful new search program and library
system in Windows 7 mean that you can forget
about where you've stored your files. To find a
missing file, just click the Start menu and type

what that file contained: a few words in a document, the name of the band singing the song, or even the year your favorite jazz albums were released.

Can My PC Still Run Windows 7?

If your PC already runs Windows Vista, it will probably run Windows 7. In fact, Windows 7 runs better on some PCs, mostly laptops, than Windows Vista does.

If your PC already runs Windows XP well, it will probably run Windows 7, but perhaps not at its best. Upgrading your PC with a few things will help Windows 7 run better. Here's the shopping list:

- **Video:** Windows 7 requires powerful graphics for its fanciest 3-D features. Upgraded video cards cost around $50, and they're not available for laptops. But if your PC's video lacks the muscle and your wallet lacks the cash, don't despair. Windows 7 simply slips into more casual clothes, letting your PC run without the 3-D views.

- **Memory:** For best results, your PC should have 1GB of memory or more. Memory's easy to install and relatively cheap, so don't skimp here.

- **DVD drive:** Unlike Windows XP, which comes on a CD, Windows 7 (like Windows Vista) comes on a *DVD*. That means your PC needs a working DVD drive to install it.

Windows 7 can run nearly any program that runs on Windows Vista, and it can run a great number of Windows XP programs. Some older programs, however, won't work, including most security-based programs, such as antivirus, firewall, and security programs. You'll need to contact the program's manufacturer to see whether it'll give you a free upgrade.

The Flavors of Windows 7

Windows XP came in two easy-to-understand versions: one for home and one for business. Windows Vista split into five different versions, each with a different price tag, and a confusing array of features. Windows 7 ups the confusion level with six versions, but the versions are much easier to figure out.

- ✔ **Starter:** This stripped-down version of Windows 7 runs mostly on netbooks — tiny PCs that lack the power for much more than Web browsing and simple word processing.

- ✔ **Home Basic:** Designed for developing countries (it isn't sold in the United States), this version contains everything from the Starter edition and tosses in better graphics, Internet connection sharing, and settings for more powerful laptops.

- ✔ **Home Premium:** Built to fill most consumers' needs, this version includes programs to let people watch and record TV on their PC, as well as create DVDs from their camcorder footage.

✔ **Professional:** Aimed at the business market, this features everything from Home Premium, as well as tools used by small businesses: **extra** networking features, for example, and similar business tools.

✔ **Enterprise:** Microsoft sells this large business version in bulk to large businesses.

✔ **Ultimate:** This version aims at the wallets of information technology specialists who spend much of their lives in front of their keyboards. If you're reading this book, you don't need this version.

Microsoft stuffs all the versions on your Windows 7 DVD, so you can upgrade at any time simply by whipping out the credit card and unlocking the features in a different version.

Being Welcomed to the World of Windows 7

Starting Windows 7 is as easy as turning on your computer — Windows 7 leaps onto the screen automatically with a futuristic flourish. But before you can start working, Windows 7 wants you to *log on,* as shown in Figure 1-1, by clicking your name.

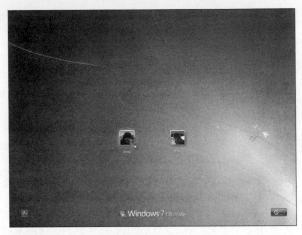

Figure 1-1: Logging on to Windows 7.

I've customized my Welcome screen. Yours will look different. If you don't see a username listed for you on the Welcome screen, you have three options:

- ✔ **If you just bought the computer, use the account named Administrator.** Designed to give the owner full power over the computer, the Administrator account user can set up new accounts for other people, install programs, start an Internet connection, and access *all* the files on the computer — even those belonging to other people. Windows 7 needs at least one person to act as administrator.

- ✔ **Use the Guest account.** Designed for household visitors, this account lets guests, such as the babysitter or visiting relatives, use the computer temporarily.

> ✔ **No Guest account** *and* **no user?** Then find out who owns the computer and beg that person to set up a username for you.

Want Windows 7 to revert automatically to this safe, password-protected logon screen whenever you leave your desk for a few minutes? After you enter your username and password, right-click on the desktop and choose Personalize. Choose the Screen Saver option in the lower-right corner and select the On Resume, Display Logon Screen check box.

Fiddling around with user accounts

Windows 7 allows several people to work on the same computer, yet it keeps everybody's work separate. To do that, it needs to know who's currently sitting in front of the keyboard. When you *log on* — introduce yourself — by clicking your *username,* as shown in Figure 1-1, Windows 7 presents your personalized desktop, ready for you to make your own personalized mess.

When you're through working or just feel like taking a break, log off so that somebody else can use the computer. Later, when you log back on, your messy desktop will be waiting for you.

Although you may turn your desktop into a mess, it's your *own* mess. When you return to the computer, your letters will be just as you saved them.

Keeping your account private with a password

Because Windows 7 lets bunches of people use the same computer, how do you stop Rob from reading Diane's love letters to Henry Rollins? How can Josh keep Grace from deleting his *Star Wars* movie trailers? Windows 7's optional *password* solves some of those problems.

To set up or change your password, follow these steps:

1. **Click the Start button and then click Control Panel.**

2. **In the Control Panel, click User Accounts and Family Safety and then choose Change Your Windows Password.**

   If your Control Panel contains dozens of icons (*way* more than the usual eight), choose the User Accounts icon.

3. **Choose Create a Password for Your Account or Change Your Password.**

   The wording that you see depends on whether you're creating a new password or changing an old one.

4. **Type a password that will be easy for you — and nobody else — to remember.**

   Keep your password short and sweet: the name of your favorite vegetable, for example, or your dental floss brand. To beef up its security level, embed a number in the password, like **3carrots** or **Ski2Alps**.

5. **If asked, retype that same password in the Confirm New Password box, so Windows knows you're not making a typo.**

6. **Type a hint that reminds you — and only you — of your password.**

7. **Click the Create Password button.**

8. **When the User Accounts screen returns, choose Create a Password Reset Disk from along the screen's left side.**

   Windows 7 walks you through the process of creating a Password Reset Disk from a floppy disk, memory card, or USB flash drive.

Once you've created the password, Windows 7 begins asking for your password whenever you log on.

✔ Passwords are *case-sensitive*. The words *Caviar* and *caviar* are considered two different passwords.

✔ Forgotten your password *already?* When you type a password that doesn't work, Windows 7 automatically displays your hint, which should help to remind you of your password. Careful, though — anybody can read your hint, so make sure that it's something that makes sense only to you. As a last resort, insert your Password Reset Disk.

Chapter 2

The Desktop, Start Menu, and Taskbar

● ●

In This Chapter

▶ Using the desktop

▶ Understanding the Start menu and taskbar

▶ Turning off your computer

● ●

*T*his chapter provides a drive-by tour of Windows 7. You turn on your computer, start Windows, and spend a few minutes gawking at Windows 7's various neighborhoods: the desktop, the taskbar, the Start menu, and the environmentally correct (and compassionate) Recycle Bin.

The programs you're using hang out on the Windows *desktop* (a fancy word for the Windows background). The taskbar serves as a head turner, letting you move from one program to another. To invite yet more programs onto the desktop, drop by the Start menu: It's full of push buttons that let you add programs to your mix.

Want to get rid of something? Dump it into the Recycle Bin, where it either fades away with time or, if necessary, can be safely revived.

Working on the Desktop

In Windows 7, your monitor's screen is known as the Windows *desktop,* and that's where all your work takes place. You can create files and folders right on your new electronic desktop and arrange them all across the screen. Each program runs in its own little *window* on top of the desktop.

Windows 7 starts with a freshly scrubbed, nearly empty desktop. After you've been working for a while, your desktop will fill up with *icons* — little push buttons that load your files with a quick double-click of the mouse.

The desktop boasts four main parts, shown in Figure 2-1.

- ✔ **Start menu:** Seen at the taskbar's left edge, the Start menu presents menus at your bidding, letting you choose what program to run.

- ✔ **Taskbar:** Resting lazily along the desktop's bottom edge, the taskbar lists the programs and files you currently have open, as well as icons for a few favored programs.

- ✔ **Recycle Bin:** The desktop's *Recycle Bin,* that little wastebasket-shaped icon, stores your recently deleted files for easy retrieval.

- ✔ **Gadgets:** Windows 7 includes small programs that stick to your desktop like magnets on a refrigerator.

Recycle Bin   Gadgets

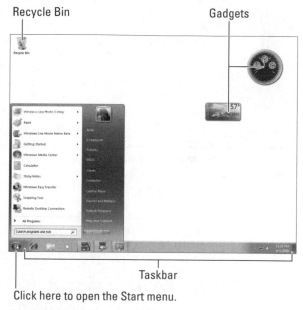

Taskbar

Click here to open the Start menu.

Figure 2-1: The Windows 7 desktop.

The following tips will help you anywhere on the desktop:

🖙 You can start new projects directly from your desktop by right-clicking the desktop, choosing New, and selecting the project of your dreams from the pop-up menu, be it loading a favorite program or creating a folder to store new files.

✔ Are you befuddled about some object's reason for being? Timidly rest the pointer over the mysterious doodad, and Windows pops up a little box explaining what that thing is or does. Right-click the object and ever-helpful Windows 7 usually tosses up a menu listing nearly everything you can do with that particular object. This trick also works on most icons found throughout your programs.

✔ All the icons on your desktop may suddenly disappear, leaving it completely empty. Chances are good that Windows 7 hid them in a misguided attempt to be helpful. To bring your work back to life, right-click your empty desktop, choose View from the pop-up menu, and make sure Show Desktop Icons has been selected.

Cleaning up a messy desktop

When icons cover your desktop, Windows 7 offers several ways to clean up the mess. If you just want your desktop clutter to look more organized, right-click the desktop, choose Sort By from the pop-up menu, and choose any of these choices:

✔ **Name:** Arrange all icons in alphabetical order using neat, vertical rows.

✔ **Size:** Arrange icons according to their size, placing the smallest ones at the top of the rows.

✔ **Item Type:** Line up icons by their *type*. All Word files are grouped together, for example, as are all links to Web sites.

✔ **Date Modified:** Arrange icons by the date you or your PC last changed them.

Right-clicking the desktop and choosing the View option lets you change the icons' size, as well as play with these desk-organizing options:

- ✔ **Auto Arrange Icons:** Automatically arrange everything in vertical rows.

- ✔ **Align Icons to Grid:** This option places an invisible grid on the screen and aligns all icons within the grid's borders to keep them nice and tidy.

- ✔ **Show Desktop Icons:** Always keep this option turned on. When turned off, Windows hides every icon on your desktop.

Dumpster diving in the Recycle Bin

The Recycle Bin, that little wastebasket icon in the corner of your desktop, works much like a *real* recycle bin. You can dump something — a file or folder, for example — into the Windows 7 Recycle Bin these ways:

- ✔ Simply right-click on it and choose Delete from the menu. Windows 7 asks cautiously if you're *sure* that you want to delete the item. Click Yes, and Windows 7 dumps it into the Recycle Bin.

- ✔ Click on the item to be deleted and drag it into the Recycle Bin.

- ✔ For a quick deletion rush, click the unwanted object and poke your Delete key.

Want something back? Double-click the Recycle Bin icon to see your recently deleted items. Right-click the item you want and choose Restore. The handy little Recycle Bin returns your precious item to the same spot where you deleted it. (You can also resuscitate deleted items by dragging them to your desktop or any other folder; drag 'em back into the Recycle Bin to delete them again.)

The Recycle Bin can get pretty crowded. If you're searching frantically for a recently deleted file, tell the Recycle Bin to sort everything by the date and time you deleted it: Right-click an empty area inside the Recycle Bin, choose Sort By, and select Date Deleted from the pop-up menu.

To delete something *permanently,* just delete it from inside the Recycle Bin: Click it and press the Delete key. To delete *everything* in the Recycle Bin, right-click the Recycle Bin icon and choose Empty Recycle Bin.

To bypass the Recycle Bin completely when deleting files, hold down Shift while pressing Delete. Poof! The deleted object disappears, ne'er to be seen again.

- ✔ The Recycle Bin icon changes from an empty wastepaper basket to a full one as soon as it's holding a deleted file.

- ✔ How long does the Recycle Bin hold onto deleted files? It waits until the garbage consumes about 5 percent of your hard drive space. Then it begins purging your oldest deleted files to make room for the new. If you're low on hard drive space, shrink the bin's size by right-clicking the Recycle Bin and choosing Properties. Decrease the Custom Size number to automatically delete files more quickly.

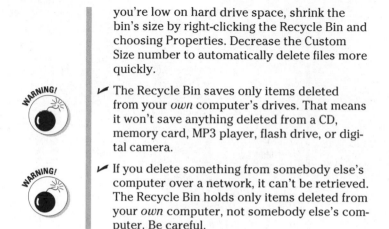

✔ The Recycle Bin saves only items deleted from your *own* computer's drives. That means it won't save anything deleted from a CD, memory card, MP3 player, flash drive, or digital camera.

✔ If you delete something from somebody else's computer over a network, it can't be retrieved. The Recycle Bin holds only items deleted from your *own* computer, not somebody else's computer. Be careful.

The Start Button's Reason to Live

The bright-blue Start button lives in the bottom-left corner of the desktop, where it's always ready for action. By clicking the Start button, you can start programs, adjust Windows settings, find help for sticky situations, or, thankfully, shut down Windows and get away from the computer for a while.

Click the Start button once, and a stack of menus pops out, as shown in Figure 2-2.

Figure 2-2: The Start button in Windows 7
hides dozens of menus for starting programs.

Your Start menu will change as you add more programs to your computer. That's why the Start menu
on your friend's computer is probably arranged differently than the Start menu on your computer.

✔ Your Documents, Pictures, and Music folders
  are always one click away on the Start menu.
  These
  folders are specially designed for their contents. The biggest perk to these three folders?
  Keeping your files in these folders helps you
  remember where you stored them and makes
  backing up your files even easier.

✔ Windows thoughtfully places your most frequently used programs along the left side of the
  Start menu for easy point-'n'-click action. And
  see the arrows to the right of some programs

listed back in Figure 2-2? Click any of those arrows to see a list of the last few files you worked on in those programs.

✔ See the words *All Programs* near the Start menu's bottom left? Click there, and yet another menu opens to offer more options. (That new menu covers up the first, though; to bring back the first, click *Back.*)

✔ Spot something confusing on the Start menu's right side? Hover your mouse pointer over the mysterious icon. Windows responds with a helpful explanatory message.

✔ Strangely enough, you also click the Start button when you want to *stop* using Windows. (You click the Shut Down button along the Start menu's bottom right, described at this chapter's end.)

The Start menu's buttons

The Start menu (shown back in Figure 2-2) comes conveniently split into two sides: one filled with icons, the other with words. The left side constantly changes, always listing the icons of your most frequently used programs. Your most oft-accessed program eventually resides atop the stack.

The Start menu's right side, by contrast, never changes. Instead, it lists these places, each one leading to a special spot in Windows:

✔ **Your Name:** The name of your user account appears at the Start menu's top-right corner. Click here to see a folder containing your most commonly opened folders.

- **Documents:** This command quickly shows the contents of your Documents library, stressing the importance of storing your work here.

- **Pictures:** Click here to see your stored digital photos and images. Each picture's icon is a thumbnail image of your photo.

- **Music:** Store your digital music here so Media Player can find and play it easily.

- **Games:** Windows 7 offers many of the same games as Windows Vista.

- **Computer:** This option displays your computer's storage areas: folders, disk drives, CD drives, digital cameras, flash drives, networked PCs, and other places that hide your Most Wanted items.

- **Control Panel:** This bundle of switches lets you adjust your computer's oodles of confusing settings.

- **Devices and Printers:** This lists your printer, monitor, mouse, and other attached gadgets to make sure they're working properly.

- **Default Programs:** Click here to control which program steps in when you open a file. Here's where you tell Windows to let iTunes handle your music instead of Media Player, for example.

- **Help and Support:** Befuddled? Click here for an answer.

- **Shut Down:** Clicking here turns off your PC. Or, click the icon's little arrow for Switch User, Log Off, Lock, Restart, Sleep, and Hibernate options.

> ✓ **Search box:** Conveniently placed directly above the Start button, this area lets you find files by typing a bit of their name or contents. Press Enter, and Windows 7 quickly dredges it up for you.

Both Windows Vista and XP listed icons for Internet Explorer and Outlook Express atop the Start menu's left edge. Windows 7 dumps Outlook Express completely and drops Internet Explorer's icon to the taskbar. To reattach Internet Explorer atop the Start menu, click the Start button, choose All Programs, right-click the Internet Explorer icon, and choose Pin to Start Menu.

Starting a program from the Start menu

This task is easy. Click the Start button, and the Start menu pops out of the button's head. If you see an icon for your desired program, click it, and Windows loads the program.

If your program isn't listed, though, click All Programs, located near the bottom of the Start menu. Yet another menu pops up, this one listing the names of programs and folders full of programs. Spot your program? Click the name, and Windows kicks that program to the front of the screen.

If you *still* don't see your program listed, try pointing at the tiny folders listed on the All Programs menu. The menu fills with that folder's programs. Don't spot it? Click a different folder and watch as its contents spill out onto the Start menu.

When you finally spot your program's name, just
click it. That program hops onto the desktop in a
window, ready for action.

If all else fails, type the program's name into the
Start menu's Search box. Type **Chess**, for example,
press Enter, and Windows' Chess Titans program
pops onto the screen, ready to crush you.

Customizing the Start menu

The Windows 7 Start menu works great — until
you're hankering for something that's not listed on
the menu, or something you rarely use is just getting
in the way.

✔ **To add a favorite program's icon to the Start
   button's menu,** right-click the program's icon
   and choose Pin to Start Menu from the pop-up
   menu. Windows copies that icon to your Start
   menu's top left column.

✔ **To purge unwanted icons from the Start
   menu's left column,** right-click them and
   choose either Unpin from Start Menu or
   Remove from This List.

When you install a program, the program almost
always adds itself to the Start menu *automatically.*
Then the program boldly announces its presence
by displaying its name with a different background
color.

You can customize the Start menu even more by
changing its properties. To start playing, right-click
the Start button, choose Properties, and click the
Start menu's Customize button. Select the check

boxes next to the options you want or deselect check boxes to remove the options. Messed up your Start menu somehow? Click the Use Default Settings button, click OK, and click OK again to start from scratch.

Bellying Up to the Taskbar

The biggest new trick in Windows 7 could be its redesigned taskbar, so pull in your chair a little closer. Whenever you run more than one window on the desktop, there's a big problem: Programs and windows tend to cover up each other, making them difficult to locate. To make matters worse, programs like Internet Explorer and Microsoft Word can each display several windows apiece. How do you keep track of all the windows?

Windows 7's solution is the *taskbar* — a special area that keeps track of all your running programs and their windows. The taskbar lives along the bottom of your screen, constantly updating itself to show an icon for every currently running program. It also serves as a dock for your favorite programs that you want to have one click away.

Rest your mouse pointer over any of the taskbar's programs to see either the program's name or a thumbnail image of the program's contents. From the taskbar, you can also perform powerful magic on your open windows, as described in the following list:

✔ To play with a program listed on the taskbar, click its icon. The window rises to the surface and rests atop any other open windows, ready for action.

✔ Whenever you load a program, its name automatically appears on the taskbar. If one of your open windows ever gets lost on your desktop, click its name on the taskbar to bring it to the forefront.

✔ To close a window listed on the taskbar, *right-click* its icon and choose Close from the pop-up menu.

✔ Traditionally, the taskbar lives along your desktop's bottom edge, but you can move it to any edge you want. (***Hint:*** Just drag it from edge to edge. If it doesn't move, right-click the taskbar and click Lock the Taskbar to remove the check mark by its name.)

✔ If the taskbar keeps hiding below the screen's bottom edge, point the mouse at the screen's bottom edge until the taskbar surfaces. Then right-click the taskbar, choose Properties, and remove the check mark from Auto-hide the Taskbar.

✔ The new taskbar has ditched the Quick Launch toolbar — a small strip near the Start button that contained icons for your favorite programs. Instead, you can add your favorite programs directly to the taskbar: Right-click the favored program's icon and choose Pin to Taskbar. The program's icon then lives on the Taskbar for easy access, just as if it were running. Tired of the program hogging space on your taskbar? Right-click it and choose Unpin This Program from Taskbar.

Shrinking windows to the taskbar and retrieving them

Windows spawn windows. To combat the clutter, Windows 7 provides a simple means of window control: You can transform a window from a screen-cluttering square into a tiny button on the *taskbar,* which sits along the bottom of the screen. The solution is the Minimize button.

See the three buttons lurking in just about every window's top-right corner? Click the *Minimize button* — the button with the little line in it. Whoosh! The window disappears, represented by its little button on the taskbar at your screen's bottom.

To make a minimized program on the taskbar revert to a regular, on-screen window, just click its name on the taskbar. Pretty simple, huh?

- ✔ Can't find the taskbar icon for the window you want to minimize or maximize? Each taskbar button shows the name of the program it represents. And if you hover your mouse pointer over the taskbar button, Windows 7 displays a thumbnail photo of that program or the program's name.

- ✔ When you minimize a window, you neither destroy its contents nor close the program. And when you click the window's name on the taskbar, it reopens to the same size you left it, showing its same contents.

Customizing the taskbar

Windows 7 brings a whirlwind of options for the lowly taskbar. First, the taskbar comes preloaded with three icons next to the Start menu: Internet Explorer (your Web browser), Windows Explorer (your file browser), and Media Player (your media browser). Like all your taskbar icons, they're movable, so feel free to drag them to any order you want.

To add more programs to the taskbar, drag and drop a program's icon directly onto the taskbar. Or, if you spot a favored program's icon on your Start menu, right-click the icon and choose Pin to Taskbar from the pop-up menu.

For even more customization, right-click a blank part of the taskbar, and choose Properties. The Taskbar and Start Menu Properties window appears, as shown in Figure 2-3.

Figure 2-3: Click the Taskbar tab to customize the taskbar's appearance and behavior.

The list below explains the window's options, as well as my recommendations for them. (You need to remove the check mark by Lock the Taskbar for some of these options to work.)

- ✔ **Lock the Taskbar:** Clicking here locks the taskbar in place, keeping you from changing its appearance. You can't drag it upward to make room for more icons, for example. Lock it, but only after you've set up the taskbar to suit your needs.

- ✔ **Auto-Hide the Taskbar:** Selecting this option makes the taskbar *automatically* hide itself when you're not near it. (Point your cursor at the taskbar to bring it back up.)

- ✔ **Use Small Icons:** This shrinks the taskbar to half-height, letting you pack in a few extra tiny icons.

- ✔ **Taskbar Location On Screen:** Your taskbar can live on any edge of your desktop, not just the bottom.

- ✔ **Taskbar Buttons:** When you open lots of windows and programs, Windows accommodates the crowd by grouping similar windows under one button: All open Word documents stack atop one Word button, for example. Choose the option called Always Combine, Hide Labels.

- ✔ **Notification Area:** This section's Customize button lets you decide which icons should appear in the notification area.

- ✔ **Preview Desktop with Aero Peek:** Normally, pointing at the strip on the taskbar's far right edge lets you behind all open windows. Selecting this check box deactivates that strip.

Feel free to experiment with the taskbar until it looks right for you. After you've changed an option, see the changes immediately by clicking the Apply button. Don't like the change? Reverse your decision, and click Apply to return to normal.

After you set up the taskbar just the way you want it, select the Lock the Taskbar check box.

The taskbar's crazy toolbars

Your taskbar won't always be a steadfast, unchanging friend. Microsoft lets you customize it even further, often beyond the point of recognition. Some people enjoy adding *toolbars,* which tack extra buttons and menus onto their taskbar. Others accidentally turn on a toolbar and can't figure out how to get rid of the darn thing.

To turn a toolbar on or off, right-click on a blank part of the taskbar (even the clock will do) and choose Toolbars from the pop-up menu. A menu leaps out, offering these five toolbar options:

- **Address:** Choose this toolbar, and part of your taskbar becomes a place for typing Web sites to visit.

- **Links:** This toolbar adds quick access to your favorite Web sites listed in Internet Explorer's Favorites menu.

- **Tablet PC Input Panel:** Meant only for Tablet PC owners, this translates pad scribblings into text.

- ↙ **Desktop:** Allows you to browse through files, folders, network locations, the Recycle Bin, and Control Panel menus by snaking your way through all the menus.

- ↙ **New Toolbar:** Click here to choose *any* folder to add as a toolbar.

Toolbars are *supposed* to be dragged around with the mouse. When the taskbar is unlocked, grab the toolbar by its *handle,* a vertical line by the toolbar's name. Drag the handle to the left or right to change a toolbar's size.

Logging Off from Windows

Ah! The most pleasant thing you'll do with Windows 7 all day could very well be to stop using it. And you do that the same way you started: by using the Start button. You then use the button resting in the bottom right-hand corner of the Start menu.

Click the Shut Down button when nobody else will be using the computer until the next morning. Windows 7 saves everything and turns off your computer.

When you're not ready to shut down, though, click the little arrow next to the Shut Down button to choose from alternatives:

- ↙ **Switch User:** Choose this option if somebody else just wants to borrow the computer for a few minutes.

✔ **Log Off:** When you're through working at the PC and somebody else wants a go at it, choose Log Off instead of Switch User.

✔ **Lock:** Meant for whenever you take short trips to the water cooler, this option locks your PC and places your user account picture on the screen. When you return, type your password, and Windows 7 displays your desktop as you left it.

✔ **Restart:** Choose this option when Windows 7 screws something up (for instance, a program crashes, or Windows seems to be acting awfully weird). Windows 7 turns off and reloads itself, hopefully feeling refreshed.

✔ **Sleep:** This option saves your work in your PC's memory *and* its hard drive, and then lets your PC slumber in a low-power state. When you return to your PC, Windows 7 quickly presents your desktop, programs, and windows as if you'd never left.

✔ **Hibernate:** Found on some laptops, this option copies your work to your hard drive and then turns off your PC — a process requiring more battery power than Sleep mode.

When you tell Windows 7 that you want to quit, it searches through all your open windows to see whether you've saved all your work. If it finds any work you've forgotten to save, it lets you know so that you can click the OK button to save it. Whew!

You don't *have* to shut down Windows 7. In fact, some experts leave their computers turned on all the time. However, *everybody* says to turn off your monitor when you're done working.

Don't just press your PC's Off button to turn off your PC. Instead, be sure to shut down Windows 7 through one of its official Off options: Sleep, Hibernate, or Shut Down. Otherwise, Windows 7 can't properly prepare your computer for the dramatic event, leading to future troubles.

Chapter 3

Navigating the Windows 7 Interface

In This Chapter

▶ **Understanding** a window's parts

▶ Understanding the new Navigation Pane

▶ Moving windows and changing their size

*T*his chapter is for curious Windows anatomy students. You know who you are — you're the one who sees all those new buttons, borders, and balloons scattered throughout Windows 7 and wonders what would happen if you just clicked that little thing over there.

This chapter dissects a typical Windows 7 window, showing you how to utilize the title bar, navigate with the Address Bar, and use the Navigation Pane. You also find out how to move windows around the desktop to better suit your needs.

Dissecting a Typical Window

Figure 3-1 places a typical window on the slab, with all its parts labeled. You might recognize the window as your Documents library, that storage tank for most of your work.

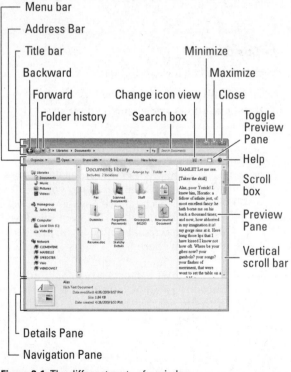

Menu bar

Address Bar

Title bar

Backward

Forward

Folder history

Change icon view

Search box

Minimize

Maximize

Close

Toggle Preview Pane

Help

Scroll box

Preview Pane

Vertical scroll bar

Details Pane

Navigation Pane

Figure 3-1: The different parts of a window.

Just as boxers grimace differently depending on where they've been punched, windows behave differently depending on where they've been clicked. The next few sections describe the main parts of the Documents library window in Figure 3-1, how to click them, and how Windows jerks in response.

- ✔ Windows 7 is full of little weird-shaped buttons, borders, and boxes. You don't need to remember all their names, although it would give you a leg up on figuring out Windows' scholarly Help menus. When you spot an odd portion of a window, just return to this chapter, look up its name in Figure 3-1, and read its explanation.

- ✔ You can deal with most things in Windows by simply clicking, double-clicking, or right-clicking; when in doubt, always right-click.

- ✔ After you click a few windows a few times, you realize how easy it is to boss them around. The hard part is finding the right controls for the *first* time.

Tugging on a window's title bar

Found atop nearly every window, the title bar usually lists the program name and the file it's currently working on. Although mild-mannered, the mundane title bar holds hidden powers:

- ✔ Title bars make convenient handles for moving windows around your desktop. Point at a blank part of the title bar, hold down the mouse button, and move the mouse around: The window follows along as you move your mouse. Let go of the mouse button, and the window sets up camp in its new spot.

✔ Double-click a blank portion of the title bar and the window fills the entire screen. Double-click it again and the window retreats to its original size.

✔ See the cluster of little icons in the WordPad program's top-left corner? New to Windows 7, those icons form the Quick Access Toolbar, and it's part of what Microsoft calls a *Ribbon interface*. Don't like the Quick Access Toolbar up there? Right-click one of the Quick Access Toolbar's icons and choose Show Quick Access Toolbar below the Ribbon.

✔ In Windows XP, every title bar carried a, uh, title of what you were viewing. Windows Vista and Windows 7, however, leave their folders' names *off* their title bars, preferring an empty strip (refer to Figure 3-1). But although many of the Windows 7 title bars lack titles, they work like regular title bars: Feel free to drag them around your desktop, just as you did in Windows XP.

✔ The right end of the title bar contains three square buttons. From left to right, they let you Minimize, Restore (or Maximize), or Close a window, topics all covered in the "Maneuvering Windows Around the Desktop" section, later in this chapter.

✔ To find the window you're currently working on, look for a darker title bar sporting a red Close button in its top-right corner. Those colors distinguish that window from windows you *aren't* working on. By glancing at all the title bars on the screen, you can tell which window is awake and accepting anything you type.

Navigating folders with a window's Address Bar

Directly beneath every folder's title bar lives the *Address Bar,* shown atop the Documents folder in Figure 3-2. Internet Explorer veterans will experience déjà vu: The Windows 7 Address Bar is lifted straight from the top of Internet Explorer and glued atop every folder.

Figure 3-2: An Address Bar.

The Address Bar's three main parts, described from left to right in the following list, perform three different duties:

- **Backward and Forward buttons:** These two arrows keep track as you forage through your PC's folders. The Backward button backtracks to the folder you just visited. The Forward button brings you back. (Click the miniscule arrow to the right of the Forward arrow to see a list of places you've visited previously.)

- **Address Bar:** Displays your current folder's address — its location inside your PC.

- **Search box:** In another rip-off from Internet Explorer, every Windows 7 folder sports a Search box. Instead of searching the Internet, though, it rummages through your folder's contents.

In the Address Bar shown back in Figure 3-2, notice the little arrows between the words *Libraries, Documents,* and *Stuff.* The arrows offer quick trips to other folders. Click any arrow and a little menu drops down letting you jump to any other folder inside that folder.

Quick shortcuts with the Navigation Pane

Windows 7 gathers up your PC's most frequently used items and places them in the new Navigation Pane. Found along the left edge of every folder, the Navigation Pane contains five main sections: Favorites, Libraries, Homegroup, Computer, and Network. Click any of those sections and the window's right side shows you the contents of what you've clicked on.

Here's a more detailed description of each part of the Navigation Pane:

✔ **Favorites:** Not to be confused with your favorite Web sites in Internet Explorer, the Favorites in the Navigation Pane are words serving as clickable shortcuts to your most frequently accessed locations in Windows:

• **Desktop:** Your Windows desktop, believe it or not, is actually a folder that's always spread open across your monitor. Clicking Desktop under Favorites shows you the contents of your desktop. (Windows 7 tosses in a few extra icons for other handy spots, including the Recycle Bin, Control Panel, and your user account folder.)

- **Downloads:** Click this shortcut to find the files you've downloaded with Internet Explorer while browsing the Internet.

- **Recent Places:** Clicking this shortcut lists every folder or setting you've recently visited.

✔ **Libraries:** Unlike normal folders, libraries show you the contents of several folders, all collected in one place for easy viewing. Windows' libraries begin by showing the contents of two folders: your *own* folder and its *public* equivalent, which is available to anyone with an account on your PC.

- **Documents:** This opens the Documents library, which immediately displays your My Documents and Public Documents folders.

- **Music:** Yep, this shortcut jumps straight to your Music library, where double-clicking on a song starts it playing through your PC's speaker.

- **Pictures:** This shortcut opens your Pictures library, the living quarters for all your digital photos.

- **Videos:** Yep, this shortcut jumps straight to your Video library, where double-clicking on a video sends the film to Media Player for viewing.

✔ **Homegroup:** New to Windows 7, Homegroups are two or more PCs that share information through a simple network. Click Homegroup in the Navigation Pane to see folders shared by other networked PCs in your Homegroup.

✔ **Computer:** Opened mainly by PC techies, this button lets you browse through your PC's folders and disks.

✔ **Network:** Although Homegroups are the rage in Windows 7, full-blown networks still work, and any networked PCs — including your Homegroup buddies — appear here.

Here are a few tips for making the most of your Navigation Pane:

✔ Feel free to add your own favorite places to the Navigation Pane's Favorites area: Drag and drop folders onto the word Favorites, and they turn into clickable shortcuts.

✔ Turn off the Navigation Pane by clicking its Organize button, choosing Layout, and then choosing Navigation Pane from the pop-up menu.

✔ Messed up your Favorites or Libraries area? Tell Windows 7 to repair the damage by right-clicking either one and choosing Restore.

Maneuvering Windows around the Desktop

A terrible dealer at the poker table, Windows 7 tosses windows around your desktop in a seemingly random way. Programs cover each other or sometimes dangle off the desktop. This section shows you how to gather all your windows into a neat pile, placing your favorite window on the top of the stack. If you prefer, lay them all down like a poker hand. As an added bonus, you can change their size, making them open to any size you want, automatically.

Moving a window to the top of the pile

Windows 7 says the window at the top of the pile getting all the attention is called the *active* window. The active window is also the one that receives any keystrokes you or your cat happen to type. You can move a window to the top of the pile so that it's active in any of several ways:

- ✔ Move the mouse pointer until it hovers over any portion of your desired window, and then click the mouse button.

- ✔ On the taskbar, click the button for the window you want.

- ✔ Hold down the Alt key and keep tapping the Tab key. A small window pops up, displaying a thumbnail of each open window on your desktop. When your press of the Tab key highlights your favorite window, let go of the Alt key.

- ✔ On newer PCs, hold down the Windows key (the one with the Windows symbol) and keep tapping the Tab key. A 3-D view of your open windows appears. When your tap o' the Tab key brings your window to the forefront, let go of the Windows key.

Repeat the process when necessary to bring other windows to the front. (And if you want to put two windows on the screen at the same time, read the "Placing two windows side by side" section, later in this chapter.)

Is your desktop too cluttered for you to work comfortably in your current window? Then drag the window's title bar to the left and right, giving it a few quick shakes; Windows 7 drops the other windows down to the taskbar, leaving your main window in place.

Moving a window from here to there

Sometimes you want to move a window to a different place on the desktop. Perhaps part of the window hangs off the edge, and you want it centered. Or maybe you want one window closer to another.

In either case, you can move a window by dragging and dropping its *title bar,* that thick bar along its top. When you *drop* the window in place, the window not only remains where you've dragged and dropped it, but it also stays on top of the pile.

Making a window bigger or smaller

Like big, lazy dogs, windows tend to flop on top of one another. To space your windows more evenly, you can resize them by *dragging and dropping* their edges inward or outward. It works like this:

1. **Point at any corner with the mouse arrow. When the arrow turns into a two-headed arrow, pointing in the two directions, you can hold down the mouse button and drag the corner in or out to change the window's size.**

2. **When you're happy with the window's new size, release the mouse button.**

As the yoga master says, the window assumes the new position.

Placing two windows side by side

The longer you use Windows, the more likely you are to want to see two windows side by side. For example, you might want to copy and paste text from one document into another document. By spending a few hours with the mouse, you can drag and drop the windows' corners until they're in perfect juxtaposition.

Or you can simply right-click on a blank part of the taskbar (even the clock will do) and choose Show Windows Side by Side to place the windows next to each other, like pillars. Choose Show Windows Stacked to align them in horizontal rows. (If you have more than three open windows, Show Windows Stacked tiles them across your screen, handy for seeing just a bit of each one.)

If you have more than two windows open, click the Minimize button to minimize the ones you *don't* want tiled. Then use the Show Windows Side by Side command to align the two remaining windows.

Windows 7 offers a new way to place two windows side by side. Drag a window against one edge of your desktop; when your mouse pointer touches the desktop's edge and the window's shaded edges fill that side, let go of the mouse button. Repeat these same steps with the second window, dragging it to the opposite side of the monitor.

To make the current window fill the screen's right half, hold the *⊞* key and press the → key. To fill the screen's left half, hold the *⊞* key and press the ← key.

Making windows open to the same darn size

Sometimes a window opens to a small square; other times, it opens to fill the entire screen. But windows rarely open to the exact size you want. Until you discover this trick, that is: When you *manually* adjust the size and placement of a window, Windows memorizes that size and always reopens the window to that same size. Follow these three steps to see how it works:

1. **Open your window.**

   The window opens to its usual, unwanted size.

2. **Drag the window's corners until the window is the exact size and in the exact location you want. Let go of the mouse to drop the corner into its new position.**

   Be sure to resize the window *manually* by dragging its corners or edges with the mouse. Simply clicking the Maximize button won't work.

3. **Immediately close the window.**

   Windows memorizes the size and placement of a window at the time it was last closed. When you open that window again, it should open to the same size you last left it. But the changes you make apply only to the program you made them in. For example, changes made to the Internet Explorer window will only be remembered for *Internet Explorer,* not for other programs you open.

Most windows follow these sizing rules, but a few renegades from other programs may misbehave. Feel free to complain to the manufacturers.

Chapter 4

Working with Folders, Files, and Programs

● ●

In This Chapter

▶ Creating, naming, and deleting folders

▶ Copying and moving files and folders

▶ Starting a program

▶ Picking a program to open a file

▶ Adding a printer

● ●

*T*he Computer program is what causes people to wake up from Windows' easy-to-use computing dream, clutching a pillow in horror. These people bought a computer to simplify their work — to banish that awful filing cabinet with squeaky drawers.

But click the little Computer icon on the Start menu, start poking around inside your new PC, and that old filing cabinet reappears. Folders, with even more folders stuffed inside of them, still rule the world. And unless you grasp Windows' folder metaphor, you may not find your information very easily.

This chapter explains how to use the Windows 7 filing program, called *Computer*. (Windows XP called the program My Computer.) Along the way, you ingest a big enough dose of Windows file management for you to get your work done.

You also find out how to launch (start) a program and dictate which program opens a particular type of file. Once you master folders and files you'll probably want to print some of your files — this chapter tells you how to install and troubleshoot a printer.

Creating a New Folder

To store new information in a file cabinet, you grab a manila folder, scrawl a name across the top, and start stuffing it with information. To store new information in Windows 7 — a new batch of letters to the hospital's billing department, for example — you create a new folder, think up a name for the new folder, and start stuffing it with files.

To create a new folder quickly, click Organize from the folder's toolbar buttons and choose New Folder when the little menu drops down. If you don't spot a toolbar, here's a quick and foolproof method:

1. **Right-click inside your folder (or on the desktop) and choose New.**

   The all-powerful right-click shoots a menu out the side.

2. **Select Folder.**

   Choose Folder and a new folder appears, waiting for you to type a new name.

3. Type a new name for the folder.

A newly created folder bears the boring name of New Folder. When you begin typing, Windows 7 quickly erases the old name and fills in your new name. Done? Save the new name by either pressing Enter or clicking somewhere away from the name you've just typed.

If you mess up the name and want to try again, right-click on the folder, choose Rename, and start over.

✔ Certain symbols are banned from folder (and file) names. You never have trouble when using plain old letters and numbers for names.

✔ Windows offers to create many more things than just a folder when you click the New button.
Right-click inside a folder anytime you want to create a new shortcut or other common items.

✔ Cautious observers may remark that their right-click menu looks different from one folder to another. There's nothing wrong; installed programs often add their own items to the right-click list, making the list look different on different PCs.

Renaming a File or Folder

Sick of a file or folder's name? Then change it. Just right-click the offending icon and choose Rename from the menu that pops up.

Windows highlights the file's old name, which disappears as you begin typing the new one. Press Enter or click the desktop when you're through, and you're off.

Or you can click the file or folder's name to select it, wait a second, and click the file's name again to change it. Some people click the name and press F2; Windows automatically lets you rename the file or folder.

✔ When you rename a file, only its name changes. The contents are still the same, the file is still the same size, and the file is still in the same place.

✔ To rename large groups of files simultaneously, select them all, right-click the first one, and choose Rename. Type in the new name and press Enter; Windows 7 renames that file. However, it also renames all your *other* selected files to the new name, adding a number as it goes: cat, cat (2), cat (3), cat (4), and so on.

✔ Renaming some folders confuses Windows, especially if those folders contain programs. And please don't rename these folders: Documents, Pictures, or Music.

✔ Windows won't let you rename a file or folder if one of your programs currently uses it. Sometimes closing the program fixes the problem if you know which one is hanging on to that file or folder. One surefire cure is to restart your PC to release that program's clutches and try again to rename it.

Getting Rid of a File or Folder

Sooner or later, you'll want to delete a file that's not important anymore — yesterday's lottery picks, for example, or a particularly embarrassing digital photo. To delete a file or folder, right-click on its name and then choose Delete from the pop-up menu. This surprisingly simple trick works for files, folders, shortcuts, and just about anything else in Windows.

To delete in a hurry, click the offending object and press the Delete key. Dragging and dropping a file or folder to the Recycle Bin does the same thing.

The Delete option deletes entire folders, including any files or folders stuffed inside those folders. Make sure that you select the correct folder before you choose Delete.

✔ After you choose Delete, Windows tosses a box in your face, asking whether you're *sure.* If you're sure, click Yes. If you're tired of Windows' cautious questioning, right-click on the Recycle Bin, choose Properties, and remove the check mark next to Display Delete Confirmation Dialog. Windows now deletes any highlighted items whenever you — or an inadvertent brush of your shirt cuff — press the Delete key.

✔ Be extra sure that you know what you're doing when deleting any file that has pictures of little gears in its icon. These files are usually sensitive hidden files, and the computer wants you to leave them alone. (Other than that, they're not particularly exciting, despite the action-oriented gears.)

- ✔ Icons with little arrows in their corner are *short-cuts* — push buttons that merely load files. Deleting shortcuts deletes only a *button* that loads a file or program. The file or program itself remains undamaged and still lives inside your computer.

- ✔ As soon as you find out how to delete files, trot off to Chapter 2, which explains several ways to *un*delete them. (***Hint for the desperate:*** Open the Recycle Bin, right-click your file's name, and choose Restore.)

Copying or Moving Files and Folders

To copy or move files to different folders on your hard drive, it's sometimes easiest to use your mouse to *drag* them there.

1. **Aim the mouse pointer at the file or folder you want to move.**

2. **While holding down the right mouse button, move the mouse until it points at the destination folder.**

   Moving the mouse drags the file along with it, and Windows 7 explains that you're moving the file. (Be sure to hold down the right mouse button the entire time.)

   Always drag icons while holding down the *right* mouse button. Windows 7 is then gracious enough to give you a menu of options when you position the icon, and you can choose to copy, move, or create a shortcut. If you hold

down the *left* mouse button, Windows 7 sometimes doesn't know whether you want to copy
or move.

**3. Release the mouse button and choose Copy
Here, Move Here, or Create Shortcuts Here
from the pop-up menu.**

Moving a file or folder by dragging it is pretty easy,
actually. The hard part is placing both the file and
its destination on-screen, especially when one folder
is buried deep within your computer.

When dragging and dropping takes too much
work, Windows offers a few other ways to copy or
move files:

- **Right-click menus:** Right-click a file or folder
  and choose Cut or Copy, depending on
  whether you want to move or copy it. Then,
  right-click on your destination folder and
  choose Paste.

- **Menu bar commands:** Click your file and then
  press Alt to reveal the folder's hidden menus.
  Click Edit from the menu and choose Copy
  to Folder or Move to Folder. A new window
  appears, listing all your computer's drives.
  Click through the drive and folders to reach
  the destination folder, and Windows carries
  out the Copy or Move command.

- **Navigation Pane:** The Computer area displays
  a list of your drives and folders along the
  bottom of the Navigation Pane. That lets you
  drag a file into a folder inside the Navigation
  Pane, sparing you the hassle of opening a destination folder.

After you install a program on your computer, don't ever move that program's folder. Programs wedge themselves into Windows. Moving the program may break it, and you'll have to reinstall it. Feel free to move the program's shortcut, though, if it has one.

Starting a Program

Clicking the Start button presents the Start menu, the launching pad for your programs. The Start menu is strangely intuitive. For example, if it notices you've been making lots of DVDs, the Start menu automatically moves the Windows DVD Maker icon to its front page for easy access.

Don't see your favorite program on the Start menu's opening list? Click All Programs near the bottom of the Start menu. The Start menu covers up its previously displayed icons with an even *larger* list of programs and category-stuffed folders. Still don't spot your program? Click some of the folders to unveil even *more* programs stuffed inside.

When you spot your program, click its name. The program opens onto the desktop, ready for work.

If your program doesn't seem to be living on the Start menu, Windows 7 offers plenty of other ways to open a program, including the following:

✔ Open Documents from the Start menu and double-click the file you want to work on. The correct program automatically opens, with that file in tow.

✓ Double-click a *shortcut* to the program.
Shortcuts, which often sit on your desktop, are
handy, disposable push buttons for launching
files and folders.

✓ If you spot the program's icon on the taskbar —
a handy strip of icons lazily lounging along your
screen's bottom — click it. The program leaps
into action.

✓ Right-click on your desktop, choose New,
and select the type of document you want to
create. Windows 7 loads the right program for
the job.

✓ Type the program's name in the Search box at
the bottom of the Start menu and press Enter.

Windows offers other ways to open a program, but
these methods usually get the job done.

On its front page, the Start menu places *shortcuts* —
push buttons — for your most-used programs. Those
shortcuts constantly change to reflect the programs
you use the most. Don't want the boss to know you
play FreeCell? Right-click FreeCell's icon and choose
Remove from This List. The shortcut disappears, yet
FreeCell's "real" icon remains in its normal spot in
the Start menu's Games folder (which hides in the
All Programs folder).

Opening a Document

Like Tupperware, Windows 7 is a big fan of standard-
ization. Almost all Windows programs load their
documents — often called *files* — exactly the
same way:

1. **Click the word File on any program's *menu bar,* that row of staid words along the program's top.**

   If your program hides its menu bar, press Alt to reveal it. Still no menu bar? Then your program might have the rule-breaking Ribbon, a thick bunch of multi-colored symbols along the window's top. If you spot the Ribbon, click the Office button in its corner to let the File menu tumble down.

2. **When the File menu drops down, click Open.**

   Windows gives you a sense of déjà vu with the Open window: It looks (and works) just like your Documents library.

   There's one big difference, however: This time, your folder displays only files that your program knows how to open — it filters out all the others.

3. **See the list of documents inside the Open dialog box? Point at your desired document, click the mouse button, and click the Open button.**

   The program opens the file and displays it on the screen.

Opening a file works this way in most Windows programs, whether written by Microsoft, its corporate partners, or the teenager down the street.

   ✔ To speed things up, double-click a desired file's name; that opens it immediately, automatically closing the Open box.

- ✔ If your file isn't listed by name, start browsing by clicking the buttons along the left side of the screen. Click the Documents library, for example, to see files stored inside.

- ✔ Puny humans store things in the garage, but computers store their files in neatly labeled compartments called *folders*. (Double-click a folder to see what's stored inside; if you spot your file, open it with a double-click.)

- ✔ Whenever you open a file and change it, even by accident, Windows 7 assumes that you've changed the file for the better. If you try to close the file, Windows 7 cautiously asks whether you want to save your changes. If you changed the file with masterful wit, click Yes. If you made a mess or opened the wrong file, click No or Cancel.

- ✔ Confused about any icons or commands along the Open box's top or left side? Rest your mouse pointer over the icons, and a little box announces their occupations.

Saving a Document

Saving means to send the work you've just created to a disk or hard drive for safekeeping. Unless you specifically save your work, your computer thinks that you've just been fiddling around for the past four hours. You must specifically tell the computer to save your work before it will safely store it.

Thanks to Microsoft's snapping leather whips, a Save command appears in every Windows 7 program, no matter what programmer wrote it. Here are a few ways to save a file:

✔ Click File on the top menu, choose Save, and save your document in your Documents folder or to your desktop for easy retrieval later. (Pressing the Alt key, followed by the letter F and the letter S does the same thing.)

✔ Click the Save icon on the menu bar.

✔ Hold down Ctrl and press S. (S stands for *Save.*)

If you're saving something for the first time, Windows 7 asks you to think up a name for your document. Type something descriptive using only letters, numbers, and spaces between the words.

✔ Choose descriptive filenames for your work. Windows 7 gives you 255 characters to work with. A file named *June Report on Squeegee Sales* is easier to locate than one named *Stuff.*

✔ You can save files to any folder, CD, or even a memory card. But files are much easier to find down the road when they stay in the Documents library. (Feel free to save a *second* copy onto your CD as a backup.)

✔ Most programs can save files directly to a CD. Choose Save from the File menu and choose your CD drive from the Navigation Pane's Computer area. Put a CD (preferably one that's not already filled) into your CD-writing drive to start the process.

✔ If you're working on something important (and most things are), choose the program's Save command every few minutes. Or use the Ctrl+S keyboard shortcut (while holding down the Ctrl key, press the S key). Programs make you choose a name and location for a file when you *first* save it; subsequent saves are much speedier.

Choosing Which Program Opens a File

Most of the time, Windows 7 automatically knows which program should open which file. Double-click any file, and Windows tells the correct program to jump in and let you view its contents. But when Windows 7 gets confused, the problem lands in *your* lap.

The next two sections explain what to do when the wrong program opens your file or, even worse, *no* program offers to do the job.

The Wrong Program Loads My File!

Double-clicking a document usually brings up the correct program, usually the same program you used to create that document. But sometimes the wrong program keeps jumping in, hijacking one of your documents. (Different brands of media players constantly fight over the right to play your music or videos, for example.)

When the wrong program suddenly begins opening your document, here's how to make the *right* program open it instead:

1. **Right-click your problematic file and select Open With from the pop-up menu.**

   Windows lists a few capable programs, including ones you've used to open that file in the past.

2. **Click Choose Default Program and select the program you want to open the file.**

   The Open With window lists more programs. If you spot your favorite program, you *could* double-click it to open your file immediately. But that wouldn't prevent the same problem from recurring. The *next* step tackles that challenge.

   If Windows doesn't include your favorite program anywhere on its list, you have to look for it. Choose Default Programs, click the Browse button, and navigate to the folder containing the program you want.

3. **Select the Always Use the Selected Program to Open This Kind of File check box and click OK.**

   That checked box makes Windows return top-billing status to your selected program. For example, choosing Paint Shop Pro (and checking the Always box) tells Windows to summon Paint Shop Pro every time you double-click that type of file.

✔ Sometimes you'll want to alternate between two programs when working on the same document. To do so, right-click the document, choose Open With, and select the program you need at that time.

✔ Occasionally you can't make your favorite program open a particular file because it simply doesn't know how. For example, Windows Media Player can usually play videos, *except* when they're stored in QuickTime, a format used by Microsoft's competition. Your only solution is to install QuickTime (www.apple. com/quicktime) and use it to open that particular video.

Adding a Printer

Quarrelling printer manufacturers couldn't agree on how printers should be installed. As a result, you install your printer in one of two ways:

✔ Some printer manufacturers say simply to plug in your printer, usually by pushing its connector into a little rectangular USB port. Turn on your PC, and Windows 7 automatically recognizes and embraces your new printer. Add any needed ink cartridges, toner, or paper, and you're done.

✔ Other manufacturers take an uglier approach, saying you must install their bundled software *before* plugging in your printer. And if you don't install the software first, the printer may not work correctly.

The only way to know how your printer should be installed is to check the printer's manual. (Sometimes this information appears on a colorful, one-page Installation Cheat Sheet packed in the printer's box.)

If your printer didn't come with installation software, install the cartridges, add paper to the tray, and follow these instructions to put it to work:

1. **With Windows 7 up and running, plug your printer into your PC and turn on the printer.**

   If your printer's rectangular connector slides into a rectangular hole or *port* on your PC, you have a *USB printer,* the type used by almost all printers today. Windows 7 may send a message saying that your printer is installed successfully, but follow the next step to test it.

   If your elderly printer's evil-looking, pronged connector pushes into a long oval connector full of holes, it plugs into your PC's *printer port.* (That connector is called *LPT1:* or *parallel* in computer language.)

2. **Click the Start menu and choose Devices and Printers.**

   The Control Panel displays its categories of devices, including your printer, if you're lucky (if your printer's name doesn't appear, though, move to Step 3). If you spot your USB printer listed by its model or brand name, right-click its icon, choose Printer Properties, and click the Print Test Page button. If it prints correctly, you're finished. Congratulations.

Test page *didn't* work? Check that all the packaging is removed from inside your printer and that it has ink cartridges. If it still doesn't print, your printer is probably defective. Contact the store where you bought it and ask who to contact for assistance.

Windows 7 lists a printer named Microsoft XPS Document Writer that's not really a printer. Choosing to print to that printer creates a special file much like Adobe's PDF files, which require a special program to view and print. Windows 7 can view or print XPS files; Windows XP, by contrast, first requires you to download and install Microsoft's XPS Viewer (www.microsoft.com/downloads).

3. **Click the Add a Printer button from the Printers window's top menu, and choose Add a Local Printer.**

4. **Choose how you've connected the printer to your PC and click Next.**

   Choose LPT1 (the oblong connector). If you're using a USB printer, click Cancel, install the printer's software, and start over. No software? You need to download it from the printer manufacturer's Web site.

5. **Choose your printer's port and click Next.**

   When Windows 7 asks which printer port to use, choose LPT1: (Printer Port).

6. **Click your printer's manufacturer and model names when you see them listed and click Next.**

The Add Printer dialog box lists the names of printer manufacturers on the left; choose yours from the list. The right side of the box lists that manufacturer's printer models. (Windows 7 knows how to talk to hundreds of different printer models.)

Windows 7 may ask you to stick the appropriate setup CD into a drive. Stuck? Click the Windows Update button; Windows 7 connects to the Internet to find software for that printer.

After a moment, you see the new printer listed. If Windows 7 offers to print a test page, take it up on the offer.

That's it. If you're like most people, your printer will work like a charm.

 If you have two or more printers attached to your computer, right-click the icon of your most oft-used printer and choose Set As Default Printer from the menu. Windows 7 then prints to that printer automatically, unless you tell it otherwise.

✔ To remove a printer you no longer use, right-click its name in Step 2, and then choose Delete from the menu. That printer's name no longer appears as an option when you try to print from a program. If Windows 7 asks to uninstall the printer's drivers and software, click Yes — unless you think you may install that printer again sometime.

✔ You can change printer options from within many programs. Choose File in a program's menu bar (you may need to press Alt to see the menu bar) and then choose Print Setup or choose Print. That area lets you change things such as paper sizes, fonts, and types of graphics.

✔ To share a printer quickly over a network, create a Homegroup. Your printer immediately shows up as an installation option for all the computers on your network.

✔ If your printer's software confuses you, try clicking the Help buttons in its dialog boxes. Many buttons are customized for your particular printer model, and they offer advice not found in Windows 7.

Troubleshooting Your Printer

When you can't print something, start with the basics: Are you *sure* that the printer is turned on, plugged into the wall, full of paper, and connected securely to your computer with a cable?

If so, then try plugging the printer into different outlets, turning it on, and seeing whether its power light comes on. If the light stays off, your printer's power supply is probably blown.

Printers are almost always cheaper to replace than repair. But if you've grown fond of your printer, grab an estimate from a repair shop — if you can find one — before discarding it.

If the printer's power light beams brightly, check these things before giving up:

✔ Make sure that a sheet of paper hasn't jammed itself inside the printer. (A steady pull usually extricates jammed paper; sometimes opening and closing the printer's lid starts things moving again.)

✔ Does your inkjet printer still have ink in its cartridges? Does your laser printer have toner? Try printing a test page: Click the Start menu and open Devices and Printers. Right-click your printer's icon, choose Printer Properties, and click the Print Test Page button to see whether the computer and printer can talk to each other.

✔ Try updating the printer's *driver,* the little program that helps it talk with Windows 7. Visit the printer manufacturer's Web site, download the newest driver for your particular printer model, and run its installation program. (I cover drivers in Chapter 12.)

Finally, here are a couple of tips to help you protect your printer and cartridges:

✔ Turn off your printer when you're not using it. Inkjet printers, especially, should be turned off when they're not in use. The heat tends to dry the cartridges, shortening their life.

✔ Don't unplug your inkjet printer to turn it off. Always use the on/off switch. The switch ensures that the cartridges slide back to their home positions, keeping them from drying out or clogging.

Chapter 5

Cruising the Web

● ●

In This Chapter

▶ Finding out about networks and the Internet

▶ Wireless connections

▶ Troubleshooting a network

▶ Setting up Internet Explorer the first time

▶ Navigating the Web

● ●

*E*ven when being installed, Windows 7 starts reaching for the Internet, hungry for any hint of a connection. After connecting with the Internet, Windows 7 kindly nudges your computer's clock to the correct time. Some motives are less pure: Windows 7 also checks in with Microsoft to make sure that you're not installing a pirated copy.

This chapter explains how to connect with the Internet, troubleshoot your network, navigate the Web with Internet Explorer, and find all the good stuff online.

Network and Internet

Windows 7 normally reaches out and touches other PCs and the Internet automatically. Plug an Internet connection into your PC, and Windows 7 quickly starts slurping information from the Web.

But should Windows 7 botch the job, turn to the Control Panel's Network and Internet category: Choose Control Panel from the Start menu and choose the Network and Internet category.

Connecting Wirelessly

Setting up your own wireless home network takes two steps:

1. Set up the wireless router or wireless access point to start broadcasting and receiving information to and from your PCs.

2. Set up Windows 7 on each PC to receive the signal and send information back, as well.

This section covers both of those daunting tasks.

Setting up a wireless router or access point

Wireless connections bring a convenience felt by every cell phone owner. But with computers, a wireless connection is more complicated to set up than a wired connection. You're basically setting up a radio transmitter that broadcasts to little radios attached to your PCs. You need to worry about signal strength, finding the right signal, and even entering passwords to keep outsiders from listening in.

Wireless transmitters, known as *wireless access points* (WAPs), come built into most routers today. Unfortunately, different brands of wireless equipment come with different setup software, so there's no way I can provide step-by-step instructions for setting up your particular router.

However, the setup software on every model of router requires you to set up these three things:

✔ **Network name (SSID):** Enter a short, easy-to-remember name here to identify your particular wireless network. Later, when connecting to the wireless network with your computer, you'll select this same name to avoid accidentally connecting with your neighbor's wireless network.

✔ **Infrastructure:** Choose Infrastructure instead of the alternative, Ad Hoc.

✔ **Security:** This option encrypts your data as it flies through the air. Most routers offer at least three types of security: WEP is barely better than no password, WPA is much better, and WPA2 is better still. Look to see which of those three acronyms your PC's wireless network adapter supports, and choose the best of the three. (Your router's security can only be as good as your wireless network adapter's security, or they can't communicate.)

Many routers include an installation program to help you change these settings; other routers contain built-in software that you access with Windows' own Web browser.

As you enter settings for each of the three settings, write them on a piece of paper: You must enter these same three settings when setting up your PC's wireless connection, a job tackled in the next section. You'll also need to pass out that information to any houseguests who want to check their e-mail on their laptops.

Setting up Windows 7 to connect to a wireless network

After you've set up your router or wireless access point to broadcast your network, you must tell Windows 7 how to receive it.

To connect to a wireless network, either your own or one in a public place, follow these steps:

1. **Turn on your wireless adapter, if necessary.**

   Many laptops turn off their wireless adapters to save power. To turn it on, open the Windows Mobility Center by holding down the Windows key and pressing X, and click the Turn Wireless On button. Not listed? Then you need to pull out your laptop's manual, unfortunately.

   If your taskbar contains a wireless network icon, click it to jump to the description in Step 3. That icon is a handy way to connect wirelessly at coffee shops, airports, and hotels.

2. Open the Start menu, choose Control Panel, choose Network and Internet, and click Network and Sharing Center.

The Network and Sharing Center window appears.

3. Choose Connect to a Network.

A window appears in your desktop's bottom-right corner, listing all the wireless networks your PC finds within range. Don't be surprised to see several networks listed, as your neighbors are probably seeing your network listed, as well.

When you hover your mouse pointer over a network's name, Windows 7 sums up the connection four ways:

- **Name:** This is the network's name, also known as its *SSID* (Service Set Identifier). Because wireless networks overlap, network names let you connect to the specific network you want. Choose the SSID name you gave your wireless router when you set it up or select the name of the wireless network at the coffee shop or hotel.

- **Signal Strength:** These green vertical bars work much like a cell phone's signal strength meter: More bars mean a stronger connection that's labeled as Excellent. Connecting to networks with two bars or less will be frustratingly sporadic, and labeled Poor.

- **Security Type:** Networks listed as Unsecured Network don't require a password. That means you can hop aboard and start surfing the Internet for free — even if you don't know who owns the network. However, the lack of a password means that other people can eavesdrop. Unsecured networks work fine for quick Internet access, but they aren't safe for online shopping. A security-protected network, by contrast, is safer, as the network's password filters out all but the most dedicated snoops.

- **Radio Type:** This lists the speed of the signal. 802.11g is fast, 802.11n is faster still, and 802.11b is slow.

4. **Connect to the desired network by clicking its name and clicking Connect.**

If you spot your network's name, click it, and then click the Connect button that appears.

If you're connecting to an *unsecured network* — a network that doesn't require a password — you're done. Windows 7 warns you about connecting to an unsecured network, but a click of the Connect button lets you connect anyway. (Don't do any shopping or banking on an unsecured connection.)

If you select the adjacent Connect Automatically check box before clicking the Connect button, Windows automatically connects to that network whenever it's in range, sparing you the process of manually connecting each time.

Clicking the two blue arrows in the upper-right corner of the screen tells Windows to search again for available networks — a handy trick when you've moved to a spot that may offer better reception.

If you *don't* spot your desired network's name, jump ahead to Step 6.

5. **Enter a password, if needed.**

When you try to connect to a security-enabled wireless connection, Windows 7 asks you to enter a "network security key" or "passphrase" — technospeak for "password." Here's where you type the password you entered into your router when setting up your wireless network.

If you're connecting to somebody *else's* password-protected wireless network, pull out your credit card. You need to buy some connection time from the people behind the counter.

Don't see your wireless network's name? Then move to the next step.

6. **Connect to an unlisted network.**

If Windows 7 doesn't list your wireless network's name, two culprits may be involved:

- **Low signal strength.** Like radio stations and cell phones, wireless networks are cursed with a limited range. Wireless signals travel several hundred feet through open air, but walls, floors, and ceilings severely limit their oomph. Try moving your computer closer to the wireless router or access point. (Or just move to a different spot in the coffee shop.) Keep moving closer and clicking the Refresh button until your network appears.

- **It's hiding.** For security reasons, some wireless networks don't broadcast their names, so Windows lists an invisible networks' name as Other Network. To connect to an unnamed network, you must know the network's *real* name and type in that name before connecting. If you think that's your problem, move to the next step.

7. **Click a wireless network listed as Other Network.**

   When asked, enter the network's name (SSID) and, if required, its password, described in Step 5. Once Windows 7 knows the network's real name and password, Windows 7 will connect.

8. **Change to a home or work network, if needed.**

   When you connect wirelessly, Windows 7 sometimes assumes you're connecting to a public network, so it adds an extra layer of security. That security makes it more difficult to share files, which is usually why you're setting up a home network in the first place.

   Fix that by switching to a home or work network: Call up the Network and Sharing Center (as described in Step 2) and then click the words Public Network — if you spot it in the View Your Active Networks section — to change the setting. When the Set Network Location window appears, choose Home Network or Work Network, depending on your location.

Choose Home or Work *only* when connecting to a wireless connection within your home or office. Choose Public for all others to add extra security.

After you've connected all your PCs, every networked PC should be able to connect to the Internet. If you're still having problems connecting, try the following tips:

✔ When Windows 7 says that it can't connect to your wireless network, it offers to bring up the Network troubleshooter. The Network troubleshooter mulls over the problem and then says something about the signal being weak. It's really telling you this: Move your PC closer to the wireless transmitter.

✔ If you can't connect to the network you want, try connecting to one of the unsecured networks, instead. Unsecured networks work fine for casual browsing on the Internet.

✔ Windows can remember the name and password of networks you've successfully connected with before, sparing you the chore of reentering all the information. Your PC can then connect automatically whenever you're within range.

✔ Cordless phones and microwave ovens, oddly enough, interfere with wireless networks. Try to keep your cordless phone out of the same room as your wireless PC, and don't heat up that sandwich when browsing the Internet.

✔ If networks leave you wringing your hands, you need a book dealing more specifically with networks. Check out *Upgrading & Fixing PCs For Dummies* (Wiley Publishing).

Troubleshooting a Network

Setting up a network is the hardest part of networking. After the computers recognize each other (and connect to the Internet, either on their own or through the network), the network usually runs fine. But when it doesn't, here are some things to try:

- ✔ Make sure that each PC on the network has the same workgroup name. Open the Start menu, right-click Computer, and choose Properties. Choose Change Settings, click the Change button, and make sure that the name WORKGROUP appears in each PC's Workgroup box.

- ✔ Turn off every computer (using the Start menu's Shut Down option, of course), the router, and the broadband modem (if you have one). Check their cables to make sure that everything's connected. Turn on the modem, wait a minute, turn on the router, wait another minute, and then begin turning on the computers.

- ✔ Right-click the network icon in your taskbar, and choose Troubleshoot Problems. The Windows troubleshooters become a little better with each new release, and the Windows 7 troubleshooters are the best yet.

Setting Up Internet Explorer the First Time

This part's easy. Windows 7 constantly looks for a working Internet connection in your PC. If it finds one, through a wired or wireless network, broadband (cable or DSL), or wireless hotspot, you're set: Windows 7 passes the news along to Internet Explorer, and your PC can connect to the Internet immediately. That means you needn't wade through this section.

If Windows 7 can't find the Internet — a frequent occurrence for people connecting through phone lines — the job's up to you, with the aid of this section.

To guide you smoothly through the turmoil of setting up an Internet connection, Windows 7 passes you a questionnaire, quizzing you about the details. After a bit of interrogation, Windows 7 helps connect your computer to your ISP so that you can Web surf like the best of them.

Here's what you need to set up a dialup Internet connection:

- ✔ **Your username, password, and access phone number.** If you don't have an ISP yet, Windows 7 finds you one, so grab a pencil and paper. (The suggested ISPs might be a tad pricey, however.)

- ✔ **A plugged-in modem.** If you're planning on connecting to the Internet through phone lines, you need a dialup modem. To see whether your PC already has a dialup modem, look for a telephone jack on the back of your computer, near where all the other cables protrude. Then connect a standard phone cable between that jack (the computer's jack says *Line,* not *Phone*) and the phone jack in your wall. No dialup modem? Buy one that plugs into your USB port, giving you a jack to plug in your phone line.

Whenever your Internet connection gives you log-on problems, head here and run through the following steps. The wizard walks you through your current settings, letting you make changes. Summon the wizard by following these steps:

1. Click the Start button, choose Control Panel, and in the Network and Internet section choose Connect to the Internet.

The Connect to the Internet window appears, asking which way you want to connect:

- **Broadband (PPPoE):** Choose this if you subscribe to one of the few broadband ISPs requiring a username and password. (Some call this Point-To-Point Protocol over Ethernet.) If you click this, enter your username and password in the boxes and click Connect to hitch up to the Internet.

- **Dial-up:** Click this if you connect to the Internet through the plain old telephone lines, then move to the next step.

- **Wireless:** If your PC has a wireless Internet adapter, Windows 7 begins sniffing out wireless signals as soon as you install the operating system on your PC.

If Windows 7 does find a *wireless* network, by chance, you're in luck. You can hop aboard the signal by double-clicking the network's name.

2. Choose Dial-Up.

If you're not choosing wireless or broadband (PPPoE), dialup is your only Internet connection option. To speed things along, Windows 7 passes you a questionnaire, ready for you to enter your dialup ISP's information.

3. Enter your dialup ISP's information.

Here's where you enter three all-important pieces of information and pick a couple more settings:

- **Dial-Up Phone Number:** Enter the phone number your ISP gave you, complete with the area code.

- **User Name:** This isn't necessarily your own name, but the username your ISP assigned to you when giving you the account. (It's often the first part of your e-mail address, as well.)

- **Password:** Type your password here. To make sure that you're entering your password correctly, select the Show Characters check box. Then deselect the check box when you've entered the password without typos.

Be sure to select the Remember This Password check box. That keeps you from reentering your name and password each time you want to dial the Internet. (*Don't* select that check box if you don't want your roommate or others to be able to dial your connection.)

- **Connection Name:** Windows 7 names your connection *Dial-Up Connection*. Change it to something more descriptive if you're juggling dialup accounts from several ISPs.

- **Allow Other People to Use This Connection:** Check this option to let people with other user accounts on your PC log on with this connection.

Clicking the I Don't Have an ISP link brings up a window where you can insert a setup CD given to you by your ISP.

Click the Dialing Rules link, next to the phone number. There, you can enter key details like your country, area code, and whether you need to dial a number to reach an outside line. Windows remembers this information, making sure that it dials a 1 if you're dialing outside your area code, for example. Laptoppers should visit Dialing Rules for every city they visit.

4. Click the Connect button.

Your PC connects to the Internet. To test your connection, load Internet Explorer from the Start menu, if it's not already loaded, and see if it lets you visit Web sites.

In the future, connect to the Internet by simply loading Internet Explorer. Your PC automatically dials the Internet using the connection you've created here.

Don't be afraid to bug your ISP for help. Most ISPs come with technical support lines. A member of the support staff can talk you through the installation process. Don't stick with an ISP that's unfriendly or that won't help you connect.

Sometimes Internet Explorer doesn't automatically hang up the phone when you're done browsing. To make your PC hang up when you close Internet Explorer, choose Internet Options from the program's Tools menu and click the Connections tab. Click the Settings button and then the Advanced

button. Finally, select the Disconnect When
Connection May No Longer Be Needed check box
and click OK.

Navigating the Web with Internet Explorer 8

Your Web browser is your Internet surfboard — your
transportation to the Internet's millions of Web sites.
Internet Explorer comes free with Windows 7 so many
people use it out of convenience. Other people prefer
browsers published by other software companies,
such as Mozilla's Firefox (www.getfirefox.com).

Simply put, you're not forced to stick with Internet
Explorer 8, the version of Internet Explorer intro-
duced in Windows 7. Feel free to try competing
Web browsers, as they all do pretty much the same
thing: take you from one Web site to another.

Moving from Web page to Web page

All browsers work basically the same way. Every
Web page comes with a specific address, just like
houses do. Internet Explorer lets you move between
pages in three different ways:

 ✔ By pointing and clicking a button or link that
   automatically whisks you away to another page

✓ By typing a complicated string of code words (the Web address) into the Address box of the Web browser and pressing Enter

✓ By clicking the navigation buttons on the browser's toolbar, which is usually at the top of the screen

Clicking links

The first way is the easiest. Look for *links* — highlighted words or pictures on a page — and click them. See how the mouse pointer turned into a hand as it pointed at the word *Books* in Figure 5-1? Click that word to see a Web page with more information about my books. Many words on this page are links, as well; the mouse pointer becomes a hand when it's near them, and the words become underlined. Click any linked word to see pages dealing with that link's particular subject.

Figure 5-1: Clicking links on a Web page.

Web page designers get mighty creative these days, and without the little hand pointer, it's often hard to tell where to point and click. Some buttons look like standard elevator buttons; others look like fuzzy dice or tiny vegetables. But when you click a button, the browser takes you to the page relating to that button. Clicking the fuzzy dice may bring up a betting-odds sheet for local casinos, for example, and vegetables may bring information about the local farmers market.

Typing Web addresses in the Address box

The second method is more difficult. If a friend gives you a napkin with a cool Web page's address written on it, you need to type the Web site's address into your browser's Address box. You'll do fine, as long as you don't misspell anything.

Using Internet Explorer's toolbar

Finally, you can maneuver through the Internet by clicking various buttons on Internet Explorer's toolbar, which sits at the top of the screen.

Hover your mouse pointer over a confusing Internet Explorer button to see its purpose in life.

Downloading a Program, Song, or Other Type of File

Sometimes downloading is as easy as clicking a Web site's Click to Download Now button. The Web site asks where to save your file, and you choose your Downloads folder for easy retrieval. The file arrives in a few seconds (if you have a cable modem) or a few minutes to hours (if you have a dialup modem).

But sometimes downloading takes a few extra steps:

1. **Right-click the link pointing to your desired file and choose Save Target As.**

   For example, to download a song from a Web site, right-click its link (the song title, in this case). Then choose Save Target As from the pop-up menu.

   When you try to download a program, Windows asks whether you want to Save the File or Run It from Its Current Location. Choose Save the File.

2. **Navigate to your Downloads folder, if necessary, and click the Save button.**

   Windows 7 normally offers to save the incoming file into the same folder your last download landed in, saving you the trouble of navigating to it. But if you prefer to download it to a different place — your Music library, for example, when downloading a song — navigate to that location and click the Save button.

No matter what type of file you're downloading, Windows 7 begins copying the file from the Web site to your hard drive. A window appears to tell you when it finishes downloading, and you can click the Open Folder button to open the folder harboring your downloaded file.

✔ Before running any downloaded programs, screen savers, themes, or other items, be sure to scan them with your antivirus program. Windows 7 doesn't come with one built-in, leaving it up to you to purchase one.

✔ Many downloaded programs come packaged in a tidy folder with a zipper on it, known as a *Zip file*. Windows 7 treats them like normal folders; just double-click them to see inside them. (The files are actually compressed inside that folder to save download time, if you care about the engineering involved.) To extract copies of the zipped files, right-click the zipped file and choose Extract All.

Chapter 6

Customizing Windows 7 with the Control Panel

. . . .

In This Chapter

▶ Working in the Control Panel

▶ Altering Windows 7's appearance

▶ Dealing with hardware and sound

▶ Setting the clock, language, and region

▶ Installing or removing programs

▶ Setting accessibility options

. . . .

*A*nybody who's seen a science-fiction movie knows that robots come with secret control panels, the best of which include an emergency Off switch. Windows 7's Control Panel lives in plain sight, thankfully, living one click away on the Start menu.

Inside the Control Panel, you can find hundreds of switches and options that let you customize the look, feel, and vibe of Windows 7. This chapter explains the switches and sliders you'll want to tweak. It also shows you how to customize Windows 7's appearance, adjust the volume, add and remove programs, and make accessibility settings.

I also list shortcuts that whisk you directly to the right Control Panel setting, bypassing the long, twisting corridors of menus. Still can't find a setting? Type its name in the Control Panel's Search box that lives in the window's upper-right corner.

One word of caution, however: Some of the Control Panel's settings can be changed only by the person holding the almighty Administrator account — usually the computer's owner. If Windows 7 refuses to open the Control Panel's hatch, call the PC's owner for help.

Finding the Right Switch in the Control Panel

Flip open the Start menu and choose the Control Panel, and you can while away an entire work week opening icons and flipping switches to fine-tune Windows 7. Part of the attraction comes from the Control Panel's magnitude: It houses more than *50* icons, and some icons summon menus with more than two dozen settings and tasks.

To save you from searching aimlessly for the right switch, the Control Panel lumps similar items together in its Category view, shown in Figure 6-1.

Below each category's name live shortcuts for that category's most popular offerings. The System and Security category icon, for example, offers shortcuts to check for the latest security updates, as well as to evaluate your PC's current security status.

Some controls don't fall neatly into categories, and others merely serve as shortcuts to settings found elsewhere. To see these and every other icon the Control Panel offers, choose either Large Icons or Small Icons from the View By drop-down list in the top-right corner of Figure 6-1. The window quickly displays *all* umpteen-zillion Control Panel icons. (To pack them all into one window, choose Small Icons.)

Figure 6-1: Windows 7 makes settings easier to find by grouping them into categories.

 Don't think something's astray if your Control Panel differs from the one in Figure 5-1. Different programs, accessories, and computer models often add their own icons to the Control Panel. Different versions of Windows 7 also leave out some of the icons seen here.

 Rest your mouse pointer over any confusing icon or category in the Control Panel, and Windows 7 thoughtfully explains its meaning in life.

 The Control Panel gathers all of Windows 7's main switches into one well-stocked panel, but it's certainly not the only way to change Windows 7's settings. You can almost always jump to these same settings by right-clicking the item you want to change — be it your desktop, Start menu, or a folder — and choosing Properties from the pop-up menu.

Changing Windows 7's Appearance (Appearance and Personalization)

One of the most popular Control Panel categories, Appearance and Personalization, lets you change the look, feel, and behavior of Windows 7 in a wide variety of ways. Inside the category await these seven options:

- ✔ **Personalization:** This area lets you stamp your own look and feel across Windows. Hang a new picture or digital photo across your desktop, choose a fresh screen saver, and change the colors of Windows 7's window frames. (To head quickly to this batch of settings, right-click a blank part of your desktop and choose Personalize.)

- ✔ **Display:** While personalization lets you fiddle with colors, the Display area lets you fiddle with your monitor itself. For example, it lets you enlarge the text to soothe tired eyes, adjust the screen resolution, and adjust the connection of an additional monitor.

- ✔ **Desktop Gadgets:** This area manages the miniprograms called *gadgets* that live on your desktop. (To jump quickly to this area, right-click the desktop and choose Gadgets.)

✔ **Taskbar and Start menu:** Ready to add your *own* photo to that boring picture atop your Start menu? Want to customize the taskbar living along your desktop's bottom edge? This is the area for you. (To jump quickly to this area, right-click the Start button and choose Properties.)

✔ **Ease of Access Center:** Designed to help people with special needs, this shortcut leads to the Ease of Access Center category. There, you find settings to make Windows more navigable by the blind, the deaf, and people with other physical challenges. Because Ease of Access exists as its own category, I describe it in its own section later in this chapter.

✔ **Folder Options:** Visited mainly by experienced users, this area lets you tweak how folders look and behave. (To jump quickly to Folder Options, open any folder, click Organize, and choose Folder and Search options.)

✔ **Fonts:** Here's where you preview, delete, or examine fonts that spruce up your printed work.

In the next few sections, I explain the Appearance and Personalization tasks that you'll reach for most often.

Changing the desktop background

A *background,* also known as wallpaper, is simply the picture covering your desktop. To change it, follow these steps:

Jump to Step 3 by right-clicking your desktop, choosing Personalize, and selecting Desktop Background.

1. **Click the Start menu, choose Control Panel, and select the Appearance and Personalization category.**

   The Control Panel opens to display its Appearance and Personalization category.

2. **Choose Change Desktop Background from the Personalization category.**

3. **Click a new picture for the background.**

   Be sure to click the drop-down list to see all the available photos, colors, paintings, and light auras that Windows 7 offers. To rummage through folders not listed, click Browse. Feel free to search your own Pictures library for potential backgrounds.

   Background files can be stored as BMP, GIF, JPG, JPEG, DIB, or PNG files. That means you can choose a background from nearly any photo or art found on the Internet or shot from a digital camera.

   When you click a new picture, Windows 7 immediately places it across your desktop. If you're pleased, jump to Step 5.

4. **Decide whether to fill, fit, stretch, tile, or center the picture.**

   Not every picture fits perfectly across the desktop. Small pictures, for example, need to be either stretched to fit the space or spread across the screen in rows like tiles on a floor.

When tiling and stretching still look odd or distorted, try the Fill or Fit option to keep the perspective. Or, try centering the image and leaving blank space around its edges.

You can automatically switch between images by choosing more than one photo (hold down Ctrl while clicking each one). The picture then changes every 30 minutes unless you change the time in the Change Picture Every drop-down list.

5. **Click Save Changes to save your new background.**

Did you happen to spot an eye-catching picture while Web surfing with Internet Explorer? Right-click that Web site's picture and choose Set As Background. Sneaky Windows copies the picture and splashes it across your desktop as a new background.

Choosing a screen saver

In the dinosaur days of computing, computer monitors suffered from *burn-in:* permanent damage when an oft-used program burned its image onto the screen. To prevent burn-in, people installed a screen saver to jump in with a blank screen or moving lines. Today's monitors no longer suffer from burn-in problems, but people still use screen savers because they look cool.

Windows comes with several built-in screen savers. To try one out, follow these steps:

Jump to Step 3 by right-clicking your desktop, choosing Personalize, and choosing Screen Saver.

1. **Open the Control Panel from the Start menu and select the Appearance and Personalization category.**

   The Appearance and Personalization category opens to show its offerings.

2. **Choose Change Screen Saver from the Personalization area.**

   The Screen Saver Settings dialog box appears.

3. **Click the downward-pointing arrow in the Screen Saver box and select a screen saver.**

   After choosing a screen saver, click the Preview button for an audition. View as many candidates as you like before making a decision.

   Be sure to click the Settings button because some screen savers offer options, letting you specify the speed of a photo slide show, for example.

4. **If desired, add security by selecting the On Resume, Display Logon Screen check box.**

   This safeguard keeps people from sneaking into your computer while you're fetching coffee. It makes Windows ask for a password after waking up from screen saver mode.

5. **When you're done setting up your screen saver, click OK.**

If you *really* want to extend your monitor's life (and save electricity), don't bother with screen savers. Instead, click Change Power Settings in Step 3. The resulting Select a Power Plan window lets you choose the Power Saver plan, which tells Windows 7 to turn off your monitor when you haven't touched a key for 5 minutes, and to put your PC to sleep after

15 minutes of inaction. (Lengthen or decrease the times by clicking Change Plan Settings in the Power Saver area.)

Hardware and Sound

Windows 7's Hardware and Sound category, shown in Figure 6-2, controls the parts of your PC you can touch or plug in. You can control your display here, as well as your mouse, speakers, keyboard, printer, telephone, scanner, digital camera, game controllers, and, for you graphic artists out there, digital pen.

You won't spend much time in here, though, especially coming in through the Control Panel's doors. Most settings appear elsewhere, where a mouse-click will bring you directly to the setting you need.

Figure 6-2: The Hardware and Sound category.

The Sound area lets you adjust your PC's volume, as well as connect seven speakers and a subwoofer to your PC, a feature much loved by World of Warcraft enthusiasts.

To turn down your PC's volume knob, click the little speaker by your clock and slide down the volume. No speaker on your taskbar? Restore it by right-clicking the taskbar's clock, choosing Properties, and turning on the Volume setting.

To mute your PC, click the little speaker icon at the bottom of the sliding control. Clicking that icon again removes the gag.

Windows 7 one-ups Windows XP by letting you set different volumes for different programs. You can quietly detonate explosives in Minesweeper while still allowing Windows Mail to loudly announce any new messages. To juggle volume levels between programs, follow these steps:

Right-clicking the little speaker icon next to your clock and choosing Open Volume Mixer jumps you ahead to Step 3.

1. **Choose Control Panel from the Start menu and select the Hardware and Sound category.**

   The Control Panel's Hardware and Sound area displays its tools.

2. **Double-click the Sound icon and then click Adjust System Volume.**

   The Volume Mixer appears listing each noise-maker on your PC.

3. **Slide any program's control up or down to muzzle it or raise it above the din.**

   Close the Volume Mixer by clicking the little red X in its corner.

Clock, Language, and Region

Microsoft designed this area mostly for laptoppers who frequently travel to different time zones and locations. Otherwise, you touch this information only once — when first setting up your computer. Windows 7 subsequently remembers the time and date, even when your PC is turned off.

To drop by here, choose Control Panel from the Start menu and click the Clock, Language, and Region category. Two sections appear:

- **Date and Time:** This area is fairly self-explanatory. (Clicking your taskbar's clock and choosing Change Date and Time Settings lets you visit here, as well.)

- **Region and Language Options:** Traveling in Italy? Click this category's icon and choose Italian from the Region and Language window's Format section. Windows switches to that country's currency symbols and date format. While you're at the Region and Language window, click the Location tab and choose Italy — or whatever country you're currently visiting.

If you're bilingual or multilingual, you should also visit this area when you're working on documents that require characters from different languages.

Adding or Removing Programs

Whether you've picked up a new program or you want to purge an old one, the Control Panel's Programs category handles the job fairly well. One of its categories, Programs and Features, lists your currently installed programs. You click the one you want to discard or tweak.

The next two sections describe how to remove or change existing programs and how to install new ones.

Removing or changing programs

To remove a troublesome program or change its settings, follow these steps:

1. **Choose the Control Panel from the Start menu and, in the Programs section, choose Uninstall a Program.**

   The Uninstall or Change a Program window appears, listing your currently installed programs, their publisher, size, installation date, and version number.

   To free up disk space, click the Installed On or Size column header to find old or large programs. Then uninstall those forgotten programs you never or rarely use.

2. **Click the unloved program and then click its Uninstall, Change, or Repair button.**

   The menu bar above the programs' names always displays an Uninstall button, but when you click certain programs, you may also see buttons for Change and Repair. Here's the rundown:

   • **Uninstall:** This completely removes the program from your PC. (Some programs list this button as Uninstall/Change.)

- **Change:** This lets you change some of the program's features or remove parts of it.

- **Repair:** A handy choice for damaged programs, this tells the program to inspect itself and replace damaged files with new ones. You might need to have the program's original CD handy, though.

3. **When Windows asks whether you're** *sure,* **click Yes.**

   Depending on which button you've clicked, Windows 7 either boots the program off your PC or summons the program's own installation program to make the changes or repair itself.

   After you delete a program, it's gone for good unless you kept its installation CD. Unlike other deleted items, deleted programs don't linger inside your Recycle Bin.

Always use the Control Panel's Uninstall or Change a Program window to uninstall unwanted programs. Simply deleting their files or folders won't do the trick. In fact, doing so often confuses your computer into sending bothersome error messages.

Adding new programs

Chances are good that you'll never have to use this option. Today, most programs install themselves automatically as soon as you slide their discs into your PC's drive. If you're not sure whether a program has installed, click the Start button and poke around in your All Programs menu. If it's listed there, the program has installed.

But if a program doesn't automatically leap into your computer, here are some tips that can help:

- ✔ You need an Administrator account to install programs. (Most computer owners automatically have an Administrator account.) That keeps the kids, with their Limited or Guest accounts, from installing programs and messing up the computer.

- ✔ Downloaded a program? Windows 7 usually saves them in your Downloads folder, accessible by clicking your username on the Start menu. Double-click the downloaded program's name to install it.

- ✔ Many eager, newly installed programs want to add a desktop shortcut, Start menu shortcut, *and* a Quick Launch toolbar shortcut. Say "no" to all but the Start menu. All those extra shortcuts clutter your computer, making programs difficult to find. (If any program adds these shortcuts, you can safely delete them by right-clicking the shortcut and choosing Delete.)

- ✔ It's always a good idea to create a restore point before installing a new program. If your newly installed program goes haywire, use System Restore to return your computer to the peaceful state of mind it enjoyed before you installed the troublemaker.

Modifying Windows 7 for the Physically Challenged

Nearly everybody finds Windows 7 to be challenging, but some people face special physical challenges, as well. To assist them, the Control Panel's Ease of Access area offers a variety of changes.

If your eyesight isn't what it used to be, you may appreciate the ways to increase the text size on your PCs.

Follow these steps to modify the settings in Windows 7:

1. **Choose Control Panel from the Start menu, select the Ease of Access category, and choose Ease of Access Center.**

   The Ease of Access Center appears, as shown in Figure 6-3. Windows 7's ethereal voice kicks in, explaining how to change its programs.

2. **Choose the Get Recommendations to Make Your Computer Easier to Use link.**

   Look for the link called Get Recommendations to Make Your Computer Easier to Use (shown with the mouse pointing to it in Figure 6-3). That makes Windows 7 give you a quick interview so that it can gauge what adjustments you may need. When it's through, Windows 7 automatically makes its changes, and you're done.

Figure 6-3: The Ease of Access Center contains a wide variety of ways to help users with physical limitations.

If you're not happy with the changes, move to Step 3.

3. Make your changes manually.

The Ease of Access Center offers these toggle switches to make the keyboard, sound, display, and mouse easier to control:

- **Start Magnifier:** Designed for the visually impaired, this option magnifies the mouse pointer's exact location.

- **Start Narrator:** Windows 7's awful built-in narrator reads on-screen text for people who can't view it clearly.

- **Start On-Screen Keyboard:** This setting places a clickable keyboard along the screen's bottom, letting you type by pointing and clicking.

- **Set up High Contrast:** This setting eliminates most screen colors, but helps vision-impaired people view the screen and cursor more clearly.

Choose any of these options to turn on the feature immediately. Close the feature's window if the feature makes matters worse.

If you're still not happy, proceed to Step 4.

4. **Choose a specific setting in the Explore All Settings area.**

Here's where Windows 7 gets down to the nitty gritty, letting you optimize Windows 7 specifically for the following things:

- Blindness or impaired vision

- Using an alternative input device rather than a mouse or keyboard

- Adjusting the keyboard and mouse sensitivity to compensate for limited movements

- Turning on visual alerts instead of sound notifications

- Making it easier to focus on reading and typing tasks

Some centers that assist physically challenged people may offer software or assistance for helping you make these changes.

Chapter 7

Protecting Windows 7

● ●

In This Chapter

▶ Dealing with permission warnings

▶ Assessing your safety in Action Center

▶ Staying safe on the Internet

▶ Using the Help feature

▶ Utilizing the Windows 7 troubleshooters

● ●

*L*ike driving a car, working with Windows is reasonably safe, as long as you stay clear of the wrong neighborhoods, obey traffic signals, and don't steer with your feet while you stick your head out the sunroof.

But in the world of Windows and the Internet, there's no easy way to recognize a bad neighborhood, spot the traffic signals, or even distinguish between your feet, the steering wheel, and the sunroof. Things that look totally innocent — a friend's e-mail or a program on the Internet — may be a virus or prank that sneakily rearranges everything on your dashboard or causes a crash.

This chapter helps you recognize the bad streets in Windows' virtual neighborhoods and explains the steps you can take to protect yourself from harm and minimize any damage.

Understanding Those Annoying Permission Messages

After 20 years of Windows development, Windows 7 is still pretty naive. Oh, it's much better than Vista, of course. But sometimes when you run a program or try to change settings on your PC, Windows 7 can't tell whether *you're* doing the work or a *virus* is attempting to mess with your PC.

Windows 7's solution? When Windows 7 notices anybody (or anything) trying to change something that can potentially harm Windows or your PC, it darkens the screen and flashes a message asking for permission, like the one shown in Figure 7-1.

Figure 7-1: Click No if this message appears unexpectedly.

If one of these permission messages appears out of the blue, Windows 7 may be warning you about a bit of nastiness trying to sneak in. So click No to deny it permission. But if *you're* trying to do something specific with your PC and Windows 7 puts up its boxing gloves, click Yes, instead. Windows 7 drops its guard and lets you in.

If you don't hold an Administrator account, however, you can't simply click Yes. You must track down an Administrator account holder and ask her to type her password.

Yes, a dimwitted security-guard robot polices Windows 7's front door, but it's also an extra challenge for the people who write the viruses.

Windows 7's permission screens are called *User Account Control* or *User Account Protection,* depending on the person you're asking.

Assessing Your Safety in the Action Center

Take a minute to check your PC's safety with Windows 7's Action Center. Part of the Control Panel, the Action Center displays any problems it notices with Windows 7's main defenses, and provides handy, one-button fixes for the situations. Its taskbar icon (the white flag) always shows the Action Center's current status.

The Action Center window, shown in Figure 7-2, color codes problems by their severity; a blood red band shows critical problems requiring immediate action, and a yellow band means the problem needs attention soon.

For example, Figure 7-2 shows a red band by the first item, Virus Protection. The second item, Set Up Backup, wears a yellow band.

All these defenses should be up and running for maximum safety, because each protects you against different things.

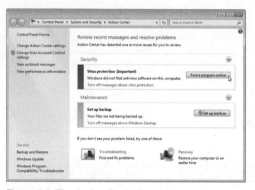

Figure 7-2: The Action Center lets you turn on your computer's main defenses.

If any of your computer's big cannons aren't loaded and pointing in the right direction, the Action Center's tiny taskbar icon appears with a red X across the flag.

When you spot that red flagged icon on your taskbar, follow these steps to visit the Action Center and fix the problem:

1. **Click the taskbar's red-flagged Action Center icon and choose Open Action Center from the pop-up menu.**

The Action Center, shown earlier in Figure 7-2, hops on-screen to display your computer's status in both security and maintenance.

Security messages: The Activity Center can show problems in any of these categories, but rarely shows more than one or two at a time:

- *Windows Update:* Windows Update program automatically visits Microsoft through the Internet, downloads any new safety patches, and installs them, all for free and all without any effort on your part.

- *Internet Security Settings:* This category covers protection settings for Internet Explorer, which help keep nasties from attaching themselves to your Web browser.

- *Network Firewall:* Windows 7's new, more powerful firewall monitors every connection arriving in and leaving your PC. When the firewall notices an unrequested connection trying to enter, it blocks it, stopping potential intruders.

- *Spyware and Related Protection:* Windows 7 includes a spyware remover called Windows Defender, and the Activity Center shouts out if it's not running correctly.

- *User Account Control:* Activity Center lets you know if something's wrong with User Account Control, and its nagging permission screens.

- *Virus Protection:* Windows 7 lacks a virus checker, but it checks to see whether you've installed one. If the Action Center notices you haven't bought an antivirus program or kept its subscription fees paid, the Action Center hoists the red flag.

Maintenance: In addition to monitoring security issues, the Activity Center monitors these three maintenance tasks:

- *Windows Backup:* Windows Backup automatically creates copies of your important files to fall back on in case of emergency.

- *Windows Troubleshooting:* When Windows notices problems with your PC or its programs, it sends up a message offering to troubleshoot them. If you clicked that message away in frustration, you can come here to take Windows up on its offer.

Don't see your previous offer of troubleshooting help? In the left pane of the Action Center window, click View Archived Messages. A window appears, listing all the offers of help Windows has given you for past problems.

- *Check for Updates:* This means Windows Update and Windows Defender have stopped checking for newly updated software.

2. **Click the button next to flagged items to fix any potential security problems.**

Whenever you notice that one of Windows 7's defenses is turned off in the Action Center, click the button next to the item. For example, in Figure 7-2, clicking the buttons named Find a Program Online and Set Up Backup will either fix the problem automatically or let you flip the right switch to set things straight.

By following thc two preceding steps, your computer will be much safer than under any other version of Microsoft Windows.

Changing the firewall settings

Just about everybody has dropped a fork to pick up the phone, only to hear a recorded sales pitch. That's because telemarketers run programs that sequentially dial phone numbers until somebody answers. Internet troublemakers run similar programs that automatically try to break into every computer that's currently connected to the Internet.

Broadband Internet users are especially vulnerable because their computers are constantly connected to the Internet. That increases the chances that hackers will locate them and try to exploit any available vulnerability.

That's where Windows Firewall comes in. The firewall sits between your computer and the Internet, acting as an intelligent doorman. If something tries to connect, but you or one of your programs didn't request it, the firewall stops the connection.

Occasionally, however, you'll *want* another computer to interact with your computer over the Internet. You may be playing a multiplayer game, for example, or using a file-sharing program. To stop the firewall from blocking those programs, add their names to the firewall's Exceptions list by following these steps:

1. **Choose Control Panel from the Start menu, click System and Security, and click the Windows Firewall icon.**

   The Windows Firewall window appears, showing the Windows 7 settings for two different types of networks you might connect with:

   - **Home or Work (Private):** Since home and work networks are more secure, Windows Firewall relaxes its grip enough to let you share files with the PCs of co-workers and family members.

   - **Public:** Public networks, like those found in coffee shops and airports, aren't secure. So, the firewall tightens its grip, forbidding the PCs around you from seeing or grabbing any of your PC's information.

2. **On the Windows Firewall window's left side, click the words Allow a Program or Feature Through Windows Firewall.**

   Windows Firewall lists every program currently allowed to communicate through its firewall. (Windows 7 adds many of its programs automatically, so don't be surprised to see a zillion programs already listed.)

3. Click the Change Settings button.

Click Continue or enter an Administrator account's password if the Windows 7 permissions screen nags you.

4. Click the Allow Another Program button, select the program (or click Browse to locate the program), and click OK.

If you click Browse, you'll find almost all of your programs living in your C drive's Program Files folder. Your program's name bears the same icon you see on its Start menu entry.

The firewall adds your selected program to its Exceptions list and begins allowing other computers to connect to it.

✔ Don't add programs to the Exceptions list unless you're *sure* the firewall is the problem. Each time you add a program to the list, you're leaving your computer slightly more vulnerable.

✔ If you think you've messed up the firewall's settings, it's easy to revert to its original settings. In Step 1, click the Restore Defaults button from the list in the window's left pane. When the Restore Defaults window appears, click the new Restore Defaults button, and click the next window's Yes button to complete the changes. The firewall removes *all* the changes you or your programs have made, letting you start from scratch.

Changing Windows Update settings

Whenever somebody figures out a way to break into Windows, Microsoft releases yet another patch to keep Windows users safe. Unfortunately, the bad folks find holes in Windows as quickly as Microsoft can patch them. The result? Microsoft ends up releasing a constant stream of patches.

In fact, the flow of patches became so strong that many users couldn't keep up. Microsoft's solution is to make Windows Update work *automatically:* Whenever you go online, whether to check e-mail or browse the Web, your computer automatically visits Microsoft's Windows Update site and downloads any new patches in the background.

When your computer's through downloading the new patches, it installs them at 3 a.m. to avoid disturbing your work. Occasionally, you're prompted to restart your computer the next morning to make the patches start working; other times, you don't even notice the action taking place.

Windows 7's Action Center explains how to make sure that Windows Update is up and running. But if you want to adjust its settings, perhaps not installing new patches until you've had a chance to review them, follow these steps:

1. **Click the Start button, choose All Programs, and choose Windows Update.**

    The Windows Update window appears.

    Not sure whether Windows Update is *really* checking for updates? Click the Check for Updates link in the window's left pane. Windows Update will drop by Microsoft to see if any updates await.

2. Choose Change Settings from the leftmost pane.

The Change Settings page appears.

3. If needed, choose Install Updates Automatically (Recommended).

Normally turned on by default, the Install Updates Automatically (Recommended) option keeps your PC updated automatically.

At this step, some experienced computer users select the option Download Updates but Let Me Choose Whether to Install Them. That option gives them a chance to ogle the incoming patches before giving the okay to install them.

4. Click OK to save your changes.

Chances are good that you won't need to make any changes. But night owls might want to change the 3 a.m. automatic installation time by clicking the drop-down lists in the Install New Updates area.

Avoiding viruses

When it comes to viruses, *everything* is suspect. Viruses travel not only in e-mail messages, programs, files and thumbdrives, but also in screen savers, themes, toolbars, and other Windows add-ons.

If you think you have a virus and you don't have an antivirus program, unplug your PC's network or telephone cable before heading to the store and buying an antivirus program. Install and run your new antivirus program *before* reconnecting your computer to the Internet. (You may need to plug in the cable while the newly installed antivirus program fetches its updates.)

McAfee offers a free virus-removal tool that removes more than 50 common viruses. Downloadable from `http://vil.nai.com/vil/stinger`, it's a handy tool for times of need.

Can't afford an antivirus program, or don't want to pay subscription fees? Check out free antivirus programs like Microsoft's Windows Security Essentials, (`www.microsoft.com/security`), ClamWin (`www.clamwin.com`), avast! Home Edition (`www.avast.com`), AVG Anti-Virus Free Edition (`http://free.avg.com`), or Avira AntiVir Personal (`www.free-av.com`). Be prepared to see some nag screens from some of these, asking you to upgrade to the paid version.

No matter what antivirus program you own, follow these rules to reduce your risk of infection:

✔ Make sure your antivirus program scans everything you download, as well as anything that arrives through e-mail or a messaging program.

✔ Only open attachments that you're *expecting*. If you receive something unexpected from a friend, don't open it. Instead, e-mail or phone that person to see whether he or she *really* sent you something.

✔ Don't install *two* virus checkers, because they often quarrel. If you want to test a different program, first uninstall your existing one from the Control Panel's Programs area. (You may need to restart your PC afterward.) It's then safe to install another virus checker that you want to try.

> ✔ Simply buying an antivirus program isn't enough. Most paid programs also require an annual fee to keep your virus checker smart enough to recognize the latest viruses. Without the most up-to-date virus definitions, virus checkers detect only old viruses, not the new ones sprouting daily on the Internet. (The newest viruses always spread most quickly, causing the most damage.)

Staying Safe on the Internet

The Internet is not a safe place. Some people design Web sites specifically to exploit the latest vulnerabilities in Windows — the ones Microsoft hasn't yet had time to patch. This section explains some of Internet Explorer's safety features, as well as other safe travel tips when navigating the Internet.

Avoiding evil add-ons and hijackers

Microsoft designed Internet Explorer to let programmers add extra features through *add-ons*. By installing an add-on program — toolbars, stock tickers, and program launchers, for example — users can wring a little more work out of Internet Explorer. Similarly, many sites use *ActiveX* — a fancy word for little programs that add animation, sound, video, and other flashy tricks to a Web site.

Unfortunately, dastardly programmers began creating add-ons and ActiveX programs that *harm* users. Some add-ons spy on your activities, bombard your screen with additional ads, redirect your home page to another site, or make your modem dial long-distance numbers to porn sites. Worst yet, some renegade add-ons install themselves as soon as you visit a Web site — without asking your permission.

Windows 7 packs several guns to combat these troublemakers. First, if a site tries to sneak a program onto your computer, Internet Explorer quickly blocks it and sends a warning across the top of Internet Explorer's screen. Clicking the warning reveals your options.

Unfortunately, Internet Explorer can't tell the good downloads from the bad, leaving the burden of proof to you. So, if you see a message and you *haven't* requested a download, chances are good that the site is trying to harm you: Don't download the program or install the ActiveX control. Instead, click one of your Favorite links or your Home icon to quickly move to a new Web site.

If a bad add-on creeps in somehow, you're not completely out of luck. Internet Explorer's Add-On Manager lets you disable it. To see all the add-on programs installed in Internet Explorer (and remove any that you know are bad, unnecessary, or just plain bothersome), follow these steps:

1. **Click Internet Explorer's Tools menu and choose Manage Add-Ons.**

   The Manage Add-Ons window appears letting you see all currently loaded add-ons.

2. **Click the add-on that gives you trouble and click the Disable button.**

Can't find the unwanted add-on? Click the Show drop-down menu to toggle between seeing All Add-Ons, Currently Loaded Add-Ons, Run Without Permission, and Downloaded Controls.

When you spot the name of an unwanted toolbar or other bad program, purge it by clicking its name and clicking the Disable button.

3. **Repeat the process for each unwanted add-on and then click the Close button.**

   You may need to restart Internet Explorer for the change to take effect.

Not all add-ons are bad. Many good ones let you play movies, hear sounds, or view special content on a Web site. Don't delete an add-on simply because it's listed in the Add-On Manager.

✔ In the rare instance that disabling an add-on prevents an important Web site from loading, click that add-on's name in Step 2 of the preceding steps and click the Enable button to return it to working order.

✔ How the heck do you tell the good add-ons from the bad? Unfortunately, there's no sure way of telling, although the name listed under Publisher provides one clue. Do you recognize the publisher or remember installing its program? Instead of scratching your head later, think hard before installing things Internet Explorer has tried to block.

✔ Don't like Internet Explorer's accelerators that show up every time you right-click inside a Web page? Dump them by clicking the Accelerators add-on category. Right-click each accelerator you don't use and choose Remove from the pop-up menu.

✔ Make sure that Internet Explorer's pop-up blocker runs by choosing Pop-Up Blocker from the Tools menu. If you see Turn Off Pop-Up Blocker in the pop-up menu, you're all set. If you see Turn On Pop-Up Blocker, click the command to turn it back on.

Avoiding phishing scams

Eventually, you'll receive an e-mail from your bank, eBay, PayPal, or a similar Web site announcing a problem with your account. Invariably, the e-mail offers a handy link to click, saying that you must enter your username and password to set things in order.

Don't do it, no matter how realistic the e-mail and Web site may appear. You're seeing an ugly industry called *phishing:* Fraudsters send millions of these messages worldwide, hoping to convince a few frightened souls into typing their precious account name and password.

How do you tell the real e-mails from the fake ones? It's easy, actually, because *all* these e-mails are fake. Finance-related sites may send you legitimate history statements, receipts, or confirmation notices, but they will never, ever e-mail you a link for you to click and enter your password. If you're suspicious, visit the company's *real* Web site — by typing the Web address by hand. Then look for the security area and forward the e-mail to the company and ask whether it's legitimate. Chances are, it's not.

Windows 7 employs several safeguards to thwart phishing scams:

✔ When you first run Internet Explorer, make sure its SmartScreen filter is turned on by clicking Safety from the top menu and highlighting SmartScreen Filter. If you see a pop-up option to Turn Off SmartScreen Filter, the filter's already turned on.

✔ Internet Explorer examines every Web page for suspicious signals. If a site seems suspicious, Internet Explorer's Address Bar — the normally white area that lists the Web site's address — turns yellow. Internet Explorer sends a pop-up warning that you're viewing a suspected phishing site.

✔ Internet Explorer compares a Web site's address with a list of verified phishing sites. If it finds a match, the Phishing Filter keeps you from entering. Should you ever spot that screen, close the Web page.

So, why can't the authorities simply arrest those people responsible? Because Internet thieves are notoriously difficult to track down and prosecute. The reach of the Internet lets them work from any place in the world.

✔ If you've already entered your name and password into a phishing site, take action immediately: Visit the *real* Web site and change your password. Change your username, too, if possible. Then contact the company involved and ask it for help. It may be able to stop the thieves before they wrap their electronic fingers around your account.

✔ You can warn Microsoft if you spot a site that smells suspiciously like phish. Choose SmartScreen Filter from Internet Explorer's Safety menu and choose Report Unsafe Website. Internet Explorer takes you to Microsoft's SmartScreen Filter Web site. Telling Microsoft of suspected phishing sites helps them warn other visitors.

✔ To find out more about phishing, drop by the Anti-Phishing Working Group (www. antiphishing.org).

Avoiding and removing spyware and parasites with Windows Defender

Spyware and *parasites* are programs that latch onto Internet Explorer without your knowledge. The sneakiest programs may try to change your home page, dial toll numbers with your modem, or spy on your Web activity, sneaking your surfing habits back to the spyware program's publisher.

Most spyware programs freely admit to being spies — usually on the 43rd page of the 44-page agreement you're supposed to read before installing the program.

Nobody wants these ugly programs, of course, so the creators do tricky things to keep you from removing them. That's where the Windows Defender program comes in. It stops some spyware from installing itself automatically and pries off spyware that has already latched onto your PC. Best yet, Windows Update keeps Windows Defender up-to-date to recognize and destroy the latest strains of spyware.

To make Windows Defender scan your PC immediately, a potential solution when your PC's acting
strange, follow these steps:

1. Click the Start menu, type Windows Defender
**into the Search box, and click its name in the
list.**

Windows Defender no longer lives on the Start
menu, like it did in Windows Vista. Nor is it
listed under any category in the Control Panel.
Unfortunately, typing its name into the Search
box is the quickest way to locate the program.

**2. Click the Windows Defender's Scan button on
the top menu.**

Windows Defender immediately performs a
quick scan of your PC. When it's through, move
to Step 3.

**3. Click Tools, choose Options, and select
the Automatically Scan My Computer
(Recommended) check box, and then click
Save.**

That schedules automatic scans to run at 2
a.m. every day, an easy way to help keep your
PC safe.

Several other antispyware programs can also scan
your computer for spyware, carefully snipping out
any pieces that they find. Some programs are free
in the hopes that you'll buy the more full-featured
version later. Ad-Aware (www.lavasoft.com)
and Spybot – Search & Destroy (www.safer
networking.org) are two of the most popular
programs.

Don't be afraid to run more than one spyware scanner on your PC. Unlike antivirus programs, antispyware programs are compatible with each other. Each does its own scan, killing off any spyware it finds.

Setting up parental controls

A feature much-welcomed by parents and much-booed by their children, Windows 7's Parental Controls offer several ways to police how people can access the computer, as well as the Internet. In fact, people who share their PCs with roommates may enjoy the Parental Controls, as well.

The Parental Controls in Windows 7 are nowhere near as comprehensive as the version found in Windows Vista. They no longer let you filter Web site viewing by categories, for example, or list the Web sites and programs accessed by your children. Instead, Parental Controls offer only these three categories:

- ✔ **Time Limits:** You can define certain hours when children (or other account holders) may log on to the PC.

- ✔ **Games:** Some over-the-counter computer games come with rating levels. This area lets you choose which rating level your children may play, helping to keep them away from mature or violent content.

- ✔ **Allow or block programs:** Don't want anybody digging into your checkbook program? This category lets you set certain programs as off-limits, while allowing access to others.

To set Parental Controls, you must own an Administrator account. If everybody shares one PC, make sure that the other account holders — the children or your roommates, usually — have Standard accounts. If your children have their own PCs, create an Administrator account on their PCs for yourself and change their accounts to Standard.

To set up Parental Controls, follow these steps:

1. **Open the Start menu, choose Control Panel, locate the User Accounts and Family Safety section, and choose Set Up Parental Controls For Any User.**

   If Windows 7's built-in policeman says, "A program needs your permission to continue," feel free to click the Continue button.

2. **Click the user account you want to restrict.**

   Windows 7 lets you add Parental Controls to only one user account at a time, a process that would have caused considerable grief for Mr. and Mrs. Brady.

   When you choose a User account, the Parental Controls screen appears. The next steps take you through each section of the controls.

3. **Turn the Parental Controls on or off.**

   The Parental Controls area first presents two switches, letting you toggle the controls between On and Off. Turn them on to enforce the rules you'll be setting up; click Off to temporarily suspend them.

4. **Choose the categories you'd like to enforce and set the limits.**

Click any of these three categories and make your changes:

- **Time limits:** This option fetches a grid, letting you click the hours when your child should be restricted from using the PC. (The clicked squares darken, representing forbidden hours. The remaining squares are fair game.)

- **Games:** You may allow or ban *all* games here, restrict access to games with certain ratings (ratings appear on most software boxes), and block or allow individual games.

- **Allow and Block Specific Programs:** Here's where you can keep the kids out of your checkbook program, for example. You can block *all* programs, or you can allow access to only a handful of programs by selecting the boxes next to their names in a long list.

5. Click OK to exit Parental Controls.

Third-party programs can add extra controls to Parental Controls, adding Web filtering, for example, to keep your children away from certain Web sites.

Consulting a Program's Built-In Computer Guru

Almost every Windows program includes its own Help system. To summon a program's built-in computer guru, press F1, choose Help from the menu, or click the little blue question mark icon. To find help in Windows Media Player and start asking pointed questions, for example, follow these steps:

1. **Choose Help from the program's menu and choose View Help. (Alternatively, press F1, or click the blue question mark icon.)**

   The Windows Help and Support program opens to its page dedicated to Windows Media Player. There, the program lists the topics that give people the most headaches.

   The Search Help box at the top of the screen lets you search the Help program's index. Typing a few words describing your question often fetches the exact page you need, saving you a few steps.

2. **Click the topic where you need help.**

   For example, clicking the Rip Music From a CD link tells Windows 7 to explain more about copying a CD's music files to your PC.

3. **Choose the subtopic that interests you.**

   After a brief explanation about the topic, the Help page offers several subtopics: You can see how to find songs copied to Media Player's library, for example, or how to edit media information like the titles of your copied songs. Don't miss the topics listed at the page's bottom; they can fetch related information you may find helpful.

4. **Follow the listed steps to complete your task.**

   Windows 7 lists the steps needed to complete your task or fix your problem, sparing you from searching through the menus of your problematic program. As you scan the steps, feel free to look at the area below them; you often can find tips for making the job easier next time.

 Confused about an odd term used in the Help window? If the term appears in a different color and sprouts an underline when you point at it with the mouse, click it. A new window pops up, defining the word.

 Try to keep the Help window and your problematic program open in adjacent windows. That lets you read each step in the Help window and apply the steps in your program without the distraction of the two windows covering each other up.

The Windows 7 Help system is sometimes a lot of work, forcing you to wade through increasingly detailed menus to find specific information. Still, using Help offers a last resort when you can't find the information elsewhere. And it's often much less embarrassing than tracking down the neighbor's teenagers.

If you're impressed with a particularly helpful page, send it to the printer: Click the Printer icon at the page's top. Windows 7 shoots that page to the printer so that you can keep it handy until you lose it.

Finding the Information You Need in Windows Help and Support Center

When you don't know where else to start, fire up Windows Help and Support center and begin digging at the top.

To summon the program, choose Help and Support Center from the Start menu. The Help and Support Center rises to the screen, as shown in Figure 7-3.

Figure 7-3: The Windows Help and Support Center offers assistance with Windows and your computer.

The program offers three sections:

✔ **Find an Answer Quickly:** This section simply reminds you to type your troublesome subject into the Search Help box along the window's top. Instead of phrasing a complete question, type just a word or two about your trouble: Type **Printer**, for example, rather than **My printer isn't working**.

✔ **Not Sure Where to Start:** If the Search Help box comes up empty, turn here. Click the How to Get Started with Your Computer link to get advice on setting up a new PC for the first time. The Learn about Windows Basics link takes you to overviews about your PC and basic Windows 7 tasks. Or, click the Browse Help Topics link to see large categories, which let you click through to more detailed information.

✔ **More on the New Windows Website:** Don't click here unless you're connected to the Internet, because this link tells the Help program to display Windows 7's online Help page at Microsoft's Web site. That site is sometimes more up-to-date than Windows 7's built-in Help program, but it uses more technical language.

The Windows Help and Support program works much like a Web site or folder. To move back one page, click the little blue Back arrow in the upper-left corner. That arrow helps you out if you've backed yourself into a corner.

Summoning the Windows 7 Troubleshooters

When something's not working as it should, the Troubleshooting section of the Windows Help and Support program may sleuth out a fix. Sometimes it works like an index, narrowing down the scope of your problems to the one button that fixes it. Then it displays the button on the Help page for your one-click cure.

Sometimes it interviews you about the problem, narrowing down the list of suspects until it finds the culprit — and your magic button to fix the situation.

Other times, a magic button isn't enough. If your wireless Internet signal isn't strong enough, for example, the Troubleshooter tells you to stand up and move your laptop closer to the transmitter.

To summon the troubleshooters, follow these steps:

1. **Right-click the Activity Center icon in your taskbar and choose Troubleshoot a Problem.**

   The Troubleshoot Computer Problems window, shown in Figure 7-4, is ready to tackle a wide variety of problems, from general to specific.

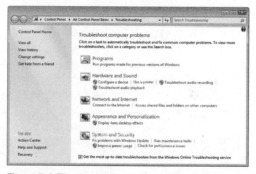

Figure 7-4: The troubleshooter programs help to solve a wide variety of problems.

2. **Click the subject that troubles you.**

   The Troubleshooting section offers these five topics that mimic their counterparts in Control Panel:

- **Programs:** This guides you through running older programs that initially balked at running under Windows 7. It also takes a look at your Web browser, and tries to fix any problems it finds.

- **Hardware and Sound:** This area shows how to diagnose driver problems, the biggest cause of bickering between Windows 7 and things plugged into or inside your PC. It also helps diagnose problems with your printer, speakers, and microphone.

- **Network and Internet:** Head here for help with Internet connections, as well as common problems encountered when connecting two or more PCs in your home.

- **Appearance and Personalization:** Can't see Windows 7's famous translucent windows? This troubleshooter checks your PC's video settings to make sure you're seeing Windows 7 in its full glory.

- **System and Security:** A catch-all section for everything else, this helps out with security and improving your PC's performance.

Click a topic, and Windows 7 whisks you to the page dealing with that subject's most common problems. Keep clicking the subtopics until you find the one dealing with your particular problem.

3. **Follow the recommended steps.**

Occasionally, you'll stumble onto numbered steps that solve your problem. Follow those steps one at a time to finish the job.

When you right-click on a misbehaving icon, you may see Troubleshoot Problems listed on the pop-up menu. Click it to fetch the troubleshooter for that particular item, saving you some time.

At the window's bottom, be sure to select the check box called Get the Most Up-To-Date Troubleshooters From the Windows Online Troubleshooting Service. That lets Microsoft add any newly developed troubleshooters to your arsenal through the Internet.

Chapter 8

Windows 7 Media Options

• •

• •

*W*indows 7's Media Player 12 is a big bundle of buttons that reveals how much money you've spent on your computer. On expensive computers, Media Player rumbles like a home theater. On cheap ones, it sounds like a cell phone's ring tone.

Media Player plays CDs, DVDs, MP3s, and videos; organizes them all into a tidy library; and can copy and burn your CDs. But because Media Player still won't work with either Apple's iTunes or Microsoft's own Zune, most folks stick with their music player's own software, leaving Media Player unclicked.

If you're curious about what Media Player can do, this chapter explains how to do those things the player can do well.

Stocking Media Player's Library

When you begin using Media Player, the program automatically sorts through your libraries' stash of digital music, pictures, videos, and recorded TV shows, automatically cataloging everything into Media Player's *own* library. But if you've noticed that some of your PC's media is missing from Media Player's library, you can tell Media Player where to find those missing items by following these steps after opening Media Player:

You can load Media Player by clicking its icon in the taskbar.

1. **Click the Organize button and choose Manage Libraries from the drop-down menu to reveal a pop-out menu.**

   The pop-out menu lists the four types of media that Media Player can handle: Music, Videos, Pictures, and Recorded TV.

2. **From the pop-out menu, click the name of the library that's missing files.**

   A window appears listing the folders monitored by your chosen library. For example, the Music library normally monitors the contents of your My Music folder and the Public Music folder.

   But if you're storing items elsewhere — perhaps on a portable hard drive — here's your chance to give the player directions to that other media stash.

3. **Click the Add button, select the folder with your files, click the Include Folder button, and click OK.**

   Clicking the Add button brings the Include Folder window to the screen. Navigate to the folder you'd like to add — the folder on your portable hard drive, for example — and click the Include Folder button. Media Player immediately begins monitoring that folder, adding its music to its library.

   To add music from even more folders or drives — perhaps a folder on another networked Windows 7 PC or a flash drive — repeat these steps until you've added all the places Media Player should search for media.

   To stop Media Player from monitoring a folder, follow these steps, but in Step 3, click the folder you no longer want monitored, and click the Remove button.

When you run Media Player, the program shows the media it has collected and it continues to stock its library in the following ways:

✔ **Monitoring your libraries:** Media Player constantly monitors your Music, Pictures, and Videos libraries, as well as any other locations you've added. Media Player automatically updates *its* library whenever you add or remove files from *your* libraries. (You can change what libraries and folders Windows 7 monitors by following the three preceding steps.)

✔ **Monitoring the Public folder:** Media Player automatically catalogs anything placed into your PC's Public folder by another account holder on your PC, or even by somebody on a networked PC.

✔ **Adding played items:** Anytime you play a music file on your PC or the Internet, Windows 7 adds the song or its Internet location to its library so that you can find it to play again later. Unless specifically told to, Windows 7 *doesn't* add played items that live on networked PCs, USB flash drives, or memory cards.

✔ **Ripped music from CD:** When you insert a music CD into your CD drive, Windows 7 offers to *rip* it. That's computereze for copying the CD's music to your PC, a task described in the "Ripping (Copying) CDs to Your PC" section, later in this chapter. Any ripped music automatically appears in your Media Player Library. (Media Player won't copy DVD movies to your library, unfortunately.)

✔ **Downloaded music and video from online stores:** Media Player lets you shop from a variety of online stores (but not iTunes). When you buy a song, Media Player automatically stocks its library with your latest purchase.

Feel free to repeat the steps in this section to search for files whenever you want; Media Player ignores the ones it has already cataloged and adds any new ones.

You'll notice a few new surprises in Media Player 12 in the form of *codecs* — the way different file formats store their music and movies. Media Player 12 recognizes more types of sound and video than before.

Unlike Media Player 11, Media Player 12 no longer offers an advanced editor for changing a song's *tags*. Instead, the player edits them for you automatically from an online database.

Browsing Media Player's Libraries

Unlike Media Player 11, which tried to integrate all its controls in one window, Media Player 12 wears two distinct faces: The Library face and the Now Playing face.

The Media Player Library window is where the behind-the-scenes action takes place. There, you organize files, create playlists, burn or copy CDs, and choose what to play. The Now Playing window, by contrast, shows what's currently playing by displaying a video or an album cover from your currently playing song. On-screen controls let you adjust the volume, skip between listed songs or videos, pause the action, or even launch multicolored kaleidoscopic visualizations while listening to music.

When first loaded, Media Player displays your Music library, appropriately enough. But Media Player actually holds several libraries, designed to showcase not only your music but photographs, video, and recorded TV shows as well.

All your playable items appear in the Navigation Pane along the window's left, shown in Figure 8-1. The pane's top half shows your own media collection, called simply Library. The bottom half, called

Other Libraries, lets you browse the collections of other people using your PC, as well as people sharing their media from networked Windows 7 PCs.

Figure 8-1: Click the type of media you're interested in browsing from the Navigation Pane along the left.

Media Player organizes your media into these categories:

- ✔ **Playlists:** Like playing albums or songs in a certain order? Click the Save List button atop your list of songs to save it as a playlist that shows up in this category.

- ✔ **Music:** All your digital music appears here. Media Player recognizes most major music formats, including MP3, WMA, WAV, and even 3GP files used by some cell phones.

- ✔ **Videos:** Look here for videos you've saved from a camcorder or digital camera, or for videos you've downloaded from the Internet. Media Library recognizes AVI, MPG, WMV, ASF, DivX, some MOV files, and a few other formats.

- ✔ **Pictures:** Media Player can display photos individually or in a simple slide show, but your Pictures library handles photos better. (Media Player can't turn photos right-side up, for example, a feat done easily in your Pictures folder.)

- ✔ **Recorded TV:** Recorded television shows appear here — if your PC has the equipment needed to record them.

- ✔ **Other Media:** Items that Media Player doesn't recognize hide in this area. Chances are you won't be able to do much with them.

- ✔ **Other Libraries:** Here, you'll find media appearing on other Windows 7 PCs in your Homegroup.

- ✔ **Media Guide:** This opens the doors to Microsoft's online music stores.

After you click a category, Media Player's Navigation Pane lets you view the files in several different ways. Click Artist in the Navigation Pane's Music category, for example, and the pane shows the music arranged alphabetically by artists' first names.

Similarly, clicking Genre in the Music category separates songs and albums by different types of music. Instead of just showing a name to click — blues, for example — Media Player arranges your music into piles of covers, just as if you'd sorted your albums or CDs on your living room floor.

To play anything in Media Player, right-click it and choose Play. Or, to play all your music from one artist or genre, right-click the pile and choose Play All.

Playing CDs

As long as you insert the CD in the CD drive correctly (usually label-side up), playing a music CD is
one of Media Player's easiest tasks. You drop it into
your CD drive, and Media Player jumps to the screen
to play it, usually identifying the CD and its musi-
cians immediately. In many cases, it even tosses a
picture of the cover art on the screen.

The controls along the bottom let you jump from
track to track, adjust the volume, and fine-tune your
listening experience.

If for some odd reason Media Player doesn't start
playing your CD, look at the Library item in Media
Player's Navigation Pane, along the left side of the
window. You should spot either the CD's name or
the words *Unknown Album.* When you spot the listing, click it and then click Media Player's Play button
to start listening.

To make Media Player automatically play your
music CD when inserted, click the Start menu,
choose Default Programs, and choose Change
AutoPlay settings. Then, in the Audio CD category,
select Play Audio CD Using Windows Media Player
from the drop-down list. Click the Save button to
save your handiwork.

Press F7 to mute Media Player's sound and pick up
that phone call.

Want to copy that CD to your PC? That's called *ripping,* and I cover ripping in the "Ripping (Copying)
CDs to Your PC" section, later in this chapter.

Playing DVDs

Media Player plays DVDs as well as CDs, letting your laptop do double-duty as a portable DVD player. Grab your favorite DVD, some headphones, and watch what *you* like during that next long flight.

Although Media Player plays, burns, and copies CDs, it can't copy a DVD's movie to your hard drive, nor can it duplicate a movie DVD. (Remember the somber FBI warning at the beginning of each DVD?)

When you insert the DVD, Media Player jumps to the screen and begins playing the movie. Media Player's controls work very much like your TV's DVD player, with the mouse acting as your remote. Click the on-screen words or buttons to make the DVD do your bidding.

To play the DVD in full-screen mode, hold down the Alt key and press Enter. Media Player fills the screen with the movie. (Hold down Alt and press Enter to revert to normal playback inside a window.) To make Media Player's on-screen controls disappear, don't touch your mouse for a few seconds; jiggle the mouse to bring the controls back in view.

Playing Videos and TV Shows

Many digital cameras can capture short videos as well as photos, so don't be surprised if Media Player places several videos in its library's Video section.

Playing videos works much like playing a digital song. Click Videos in the Navigation Pane along Media Player's left side. Double-click the video you want to see, and start enjoying the action.

Media Player lets you watch videos in several sizes. Hold down Alt and press Enter to make it fill the screen, just as when watching a DVD. (Repeat those keystrokes to return to the original size.)

- ✔ To make the video adjust itself automatically to the size of your Media Player window, right-click the video as it plays, choose Video from the pop-up menu, and select Fit Video to Player on Resize.

- ✔ When downloading video from the Internet, make sure that it's stored in Windows Media format. Media Player can't play videos stored in some QuickTime or RealVideo formats. Those two competing formats require free players available from Apple (www.apple.com/quicktime) or Real (www.real.com). Make sure that you download the *free* versions — those sites often try to sucker you into buying their pay versions.

- ✔ When choosing video to watch on the Internet, your connection speed determines its quality. If you have a dialup connection, watch the video's 56K version. Broadband users can watch either the 100K or 300K version. You can't damage your computer by choosing the wrong version; the video will just play with some skipping.

- ✔ Media Player's Recorded TV area lists TV shows recorded by Windows 7's *Media Center*. You can watch those recorded shows in both Windows Media Center and Windows Media Player.

Playing Music Files (MP3s and WMAs)

Media Player plays several types of digital music files, but they all have one thing in common: When you tell Media Player to play a song or an album, Media Player immediately places that item on your *Now Playing list* — a list of items queued up for playing one after the other.

You can start playing music through Media Player in a number of ways, even if Media Player isn't currently running:

✔ Double-click the Library icon on your taskbar, right-click an album or a music-filled folder, and choose Play with Windows Media Player. The player jumps to the screen to begin playing your choice.

✔ While you're still in your own Music library, right-click items and choose Add to Windows Media Player list. Your PC queues them up in Media Player, ready to be played after you've heard your currently playing music.

✔ Double-click a song file, whether it's sitting on your desktop or in any folder. Media Player begins playing it immediately.

To play songs listed within Media Player's own library, right-click the song's name and choose Play. Media Player begins playing it immediately, and the song appears in the Now Playing list.

Here are other ways to play songs within Media Player:

✔ To play an entire album in Media Player's library, right-click the album from the library's Album category and choose Play.

✔ Want to hear several files or albums, one after the other? Right-click the first one and choose Play. Right-click the next one and choose Add to Now Playing list. Repeat until you're done. Media Player queues them all up in the Now Playing list.

✔ To return to a recently played item, right-click Media Player's icon in the taskbar. When the list of recently played items appears, click your item's name.

✔ No decent music in your music library? Then start copying your favorite CDs to your PC — a process called *ripping,* which I explain in the next section.

Ripping (Copying) CDs to Your PC

In a process known as *ripping,* Windows 7's Media Player can copy your CDs to your PC as MP3 files, the industry standard for digital music. But until you tell the player that you want MP3 files, it creates *WMA* files — a format that won't play on iPods.

To make Media Player create songs with the more versatile MP3 format instead of WMA, click the Organize button, choose Options, and click the Rip Music tab. Choose MP3 instead of WMA from the Format pull-down menu and nudge the audio quality over a tad from 128 to 256, or even 320 for better sound.

To copy CDs to your PC's hard drive, follow these instructions:

1. **Open Media Player, insert a music CD, and click the Rip CD button.**

   You may need to push a button on the front of the drive before the tray ejects.

   Media Player connects to the Internet, identifies your CD, and fills in the album's name, artist, and song titles. Then the program begins copying the CD's songs to your PC and listing their titles in the Media Player Library. You're through.

   If Media Player can't find the songs' titles automatically, however, move ahead to Step 2.

2. **Right-click the first track and choose Find Album Info, if necessary.**

   If Media Player comes up empty-handed, right-click the first track and choose Find Album Info.

   If you're connected to the Internet, type the album's name into the Search box and then click Search. If the Search box finds your album, click its name, choose Next, and click Finish.

   If you're not connected to the Internet, or if the Search box comes up empty, right-click the first song, click Edit, and manually fill in the song title. Repeat for the other titles, as well as the album, artist, genre, and year tags.

Here are some tips for ripping CDs to your computer:

- ✔ Normally Media Player copies every song on the CD. To leave Tiny Tim off your ukulele music compilation, however, remove the check mark from Tiny Tim's name. If Media Player has already copied the song to your PC, feel free to delete it from within Media Player. Click the Library button, right-click the song sung by the offending yodeler, and choose Delete.

- ✔ Some record companies add copy protection to their CDs to keep you from copying them to your computer. If you buy a copy-protected CD, try holding down the Shift key for a few seconds just before and after pushing the CD into the CD tray. That sometimes keeps the copy-protection software from working.

- ✔ Don't work your computer too hard while it's ripping songs — just let it sit there and churn away. Running large programs in the background may distract it, potentially interfering with the music.

- ✔ Media Player automatically places your ripped CDs into your Music library. You'll also find your newly ripped music there as well as in the Media Player Library.

Burning (Creating) Music CDs

To create a music CD with your favorite songs, create a playlist containing the CD's songs, listed in the order you want to play them; then burn the playlist to a CD.

But what if you want to duplicate a CD, perhaps to create a disposable copy of your favorite CD to play in your car? No sense scratching up your original. You'll want to make copies of your kids' CDs, too, before they create pizzas out of them.

Unfortunately, neither Media Player nor Windows 7 offers a Duplicate CD option. Instead, you must jump through the following five hoops to create a new CD with the same songs as the original CD:

1. **Rip (copy) the music to your hard drive.**

   Before ripping your CD, change your burning quality
   to the highest quality: Click Organize, choose Options, click the Rip Music tab, and change the Format box to WAVE (Lossless). Click OK.

2. **Insert a blank CD into your writable CD drive.**

3. **In Media Player's Navigation Pane, click the Music category and choose Album to see your saved CDs.**

4. **Right-click the album in your library, choose Add To, and choose Burn List.**

   If your Burn List already had some listed music, click the Clear List button to clear it; then add your CD's music to the Burn List.

5. **Click the Start Burn button.**

Now, for the fine print. Unless you change the quality to WAV (Lossless) when copying the CD to your PC, Media Player compresses your songs as it saves them on your hard drive, throwing out some audio quality in the process. Burning them back to

CD won't replace that lost quality. If you want *true* duplicates of your CDs, change the Ripping Format to WAV (Lossless).

If you do change the format to WAV (Lossless) in order to duplicate a CD, remember to change it back to MP3 afterward, or your hard drive will run out of room when you begin ripping a lot of CDs.

A simpler solution might be to buy CD-burning software from your local office supply or computer store. Unlike Windows Media Player, most CD-burning programs have a Duplicate CD button for one-click convenience.

Copying Songs to Your Portable Player

Media Player 12 works with only a handful of portable music players. It can't connect with Apple's iPod, for example. It won't even work with Microsoft's own Zune. And it's clearly optimized for transferring WMA files — not the MP3 files favored by most portable players.

In fact, most people don't bother with Media Player, instead opting for the transfer software that came with their portable player: iTunes for iPods (`www.apple.com/itunes`) and Zune software for the Zune (`www.zune.com`). But if you own one of the few gadgets that Media Player likes, follow these steps:

1. Connect your player to your computer.

This step usually involves connecting a USB cord between your device and your computer. The cord's small end pushes into a hole on your player; the large end fits into a rectangular-shaped port in the front or back of your PC.

The plugs only fit one way — the right way — on each end.

2. **Start Media Player.**

Several things may happen at this point, depending on your particular music player and the way its manufacturer set it up. (Try looking for some of these options on your player's setup menus.)

If Media Player recognizes your player, a Sync List pane appears along Media Player's right edge.

If your player is set up to *Sync Automatically,* Media Player dutifully copies all the music (and video, if your player supports it) from Media Player's library to your player. It's a fairly quick process for a few hundred songs, but if your player holds thousands, you may be twiddling your thumbs for several minutes.

If your player is set up to *Sync Manually,* click Finish. You need to tell Media Player what music to copy, covered in the next step.

If your player does nothing, or Media Player's library holds more music than will fit on your player, you're forced to go to Step 3.

3. **Choose what music to stuff onto your player.**

You can choose what music goes onto your player in a couple of ways:

- **Shuffle Music:** Found in the Sync List pane, this quick and easy option tells Media Player to copy a random mix of songs to the Sync List. It's great for an on-the-fly refresher, but you give up control over exactly what music will live on your player.

- **Playlist:** Create a *playlist* — a list of music — that you want to appear on your player. Already created a playlist or two that you like? Right-click them and choose Add to Sync List, and Media Player will toss those songs onto the Sync List that's aimed at your player.

4. **Click the Start Sync button.**

   After you've chosen the music to transfer — and it's all sitting in the Sync List pane along the player's right side — copy it all to your player by clicking the Start Sync button at the bottom of Media Player's right pane.

   Media Player sends your music to your player, taking anywhere from several seconds to a few minutes.

✔ If Media Player can't seem to find your portable player, click the Sync button along Media Player's top and choose Refresh Devices. That tells Media Player to take another look before giving up.

✔ To change how Media Player sends files to your particular media player, click the Organize button, choose Options, and click the Devices tab. Double-click your player's name to see its current options. Some players offer zillions of options; others only offer a few.

> ✔ Some players may require *firmware upgrades* —
> special pieces of software — before they'll
> work with Media Player 12. Downloadable
> from the manufacturer's Web site, firmware
> upgrades run on your PC like any software
> installation program. But instead of installing
> software on your PC, they install software onto
> your portable player to bring it up to date.

Dumping the Camera's Photos into Your Computer

Most digital cameras come with software that grabs
your camera's photos and places them into your
computer. But you needn't install it, or even bother
trying to figure it out, thank goodness. Windows 7's
built-in software easily fetches photos from nearly
any make and model of digital camera when you
follow these steps:

1. **Plug the camera's cable into your computer.**

   Most cameras come with two cables: One that
   plugs into your TV set for viewing, and another
   that plugs into your PC. You need to find the
   one that plugs into your PC for transferring
   photos.

   Plug the transfer cable's small end into your
   camera, and the larger end into your computer's *USB port,* a rectangular-looking hole about
   ½-inch long and ¼-inch high. (Most USB ports
   live on the back of the computer; newer computers offer them up front, and laptops place
   them along the sides.)

2. Turn on your camera (if it's not already turned on) and wait for Windows 7 to recognize it.

If you're plugging in the camera for the first time, Windows 7 sometimes heralds the camera's presence by listing its model number in a pop-up window above your taskbar by the clock.

If Windows 7 doesn't recognize your camera, make sure that the camera is set to *display mode* — the mode where you can see your photos on the camera's viewfinder — rather than the mode you use for snapping photos. If you still have problems, unplug the cable from your PC, wait a few seconds, then plug it back in.

When Windows 7 recognizes your camera, the AutoPlay window appears, as shown in Figure 8-2.

Don't see the AutoPlay window? Try opening Computer from the Start menu and double-clicking your camera icon.

Figure 8-2: Click the Import Pictures and Videos Using Windows option.

3. **In the AutoPlay window, select the check box called Always Do This for This device and then click the Import Pictures and Videos Using Windows option.**

Selecting the Always Do This for This Device check box is a timesaver that tells Windows 7 to automatically grab your camera's pictures whenever you connect it to your PC.

After you click the Import Pictures and Videos Using Windows option, the Import Pictures and Videos dialog box appears.

4. **Type a *tag* or name for your photos and click the Import button.**

Type a word or two to describe the photos. If you type the word **Cat**, for example, Windows 7 names the incoming photos as Cat 001, Cat 002, Cat 003, and so on. Later, you can find these pictures by searching for the word **Cat** in your Start menu's Search box.

Tagging works best when all your photos come from *one* session — that rainy afternoon spent with the cat, for example.

Clicking the Import button brings your camera's photos into your PC and automatically renames them.

Clicking the words Import Settings lets you change how Windows 7 imports your photos. It's worth a look-see because it lets you undo any options you've mistakenly chosen when importing your first batch of photos.

5. Select the Erase After Importing check box.

If you don't delete your camera's photos after Windows 7 copies them into your PC, you won't have room to take more photos. As Windows 7 grabs your photos, click Erase After Importing and Windows 7 erases the camera's photos, saving you the trouble of rummaging through your camera's menus.

When Windows finishes importing your photos, it displays the folder containing your new pictures.

Browsing Your Photos in the Pictures Library

Your Pictures library, located one click away on the Start menu's right side, easily earns kudos as Windows 7's best place to store your digital photos. When Windows 7 imports your digital camera's photos, it automatically stuffs them there to take advantage of that folder's built-in viewing tools.

To peek inside any folder in your Pictures library, double-click the folder's icon. Inside, each folder offers the usual file-viewing tools found in every folder, plus a convenient row of buttons along the top for displaying, e-mailing, or printing your selected photos. (Click the View button to cycle quickly through different thumbnail sizes.)

Shown in Figure 8-3, the Pictures library offers oodles of ways to sort quickly through thousands of photos by clicking different words, dates, and ratings listed on the Arrange By drop-down list. Double-click any photo to see a larger view in Photo

Viewer; return to the Pictures library by closing the Photo Viewer with a click on the red X in the Photo Viewer's upper-right corner.

Figure 8-3: The Pictures library lets you sort through your pictures.

The options in the Arrange By drop-down list let you sort your photos in a variety of ways:

- ✔ **Folder:** The most common view, this shows your Pictures library, complete with all the folders inside it. Double-click any folder to see inside; click the blue back arrow in the top-left corner to return.

- ✔ **Month:** Handy for viewing photos taken over the long term, this option stacks your photos into piles organized by the month and year you shot them. Double-click the July 2008 stack, for example, to see all the photos you snapped in that particular month.

✔ **Day:** Click this when you want to see all the photos snapped on a particular day. The Pictures library groups them by day, with your most recent photos in the topmost group.

✔ **Rating:** Spot a photo that's a real keeper? Or perhaps a stinker? Rate your currently selected photo or photos by clicking any of the rating stars on the Details Pane, as shown along the bottom of Figure 8-3.

✔ **Tag:** Remember the tag you assigned to your photos when importing them from your digital camera? The Pictures library stacks your photos according to their tags, letting you retrieve your tagged photos with a click. Feel free to add tags on the fly: Select your photos of Uncle Frank (select several photos by holding down Ctrl as you click each one), click the Tag area in the Details Pane along the window's bottom, and type **Uncle Frank** to add that name as a tag.

By sorting dates, tags, and ratings, you can ferret out the particular photos you're after. The following tips also increase your chances of locating a particular photo:

✔ Spot a blurred or ugly photo? Right-click it and choose Delete. Taking out the garbage with the Delete key makes the good photos easier to find.

✔ You can assign several different tags to one photo, adding a tag for each person in a group picture, for example: **Barack; Michelle; Sasha; Malia**. (The semicolon separates each tag.) Adding several tags makes that photo appear in searches for *any* of its tags.

✔ Windows 7 dropped Vista's Preview Pane from the library's right edge. To replace it with Windows 7's more limited Preview Pane, click the Organize button, choose Layout, and select Preview Pane.

✔ Don't see enough details about a photo along the folder's bottom edge? Drag the Details Pane's top edge upward with your mouse, and the pane expands to show oodles of information.

✔ Type any photo's tag into the Pictures library's Search box, located in its top-right corner, and Windows 7 quickly displays photos assigned with that particular tag.

✔ Want to cover your entire desktop with a photo? Right-click the picture and choose Set As Background. Windows immediately splashes that photo across your desktop.

✔ Hover your mouse pointer over any photo to see the date it was taken, its rating, size, and dimensions. (That information also appears in the Details Pane along the window's bottom.)

Copying Digital Photos to a CD or DVD

To back up all your digital photos, fire up Windows 7's backup program. But if you just want to copy some photos to a CD or DVD, stick around.

Head to the computer or office-supply store and pick up a stack of blank CDs or DVDs to match your PC's drive. Then follow these steps to copy files in your Pictures library to a blank CD or DVD:

1. **Open your Pictures library from the Start menu, select your desired photos, and click the Burn button.**

   Open the Pictures library, and open the folder containing the photos you want to copy to disc. Select the photos and folders you want to copy by holding down the Ctrl key and clicking their icons. Or, to select them *all,* hold down Ctrl and press the letter A. When you click the Burn button, Windows 7 asks you to insert a blank disc into your drive.

2. **Insert a blank CD or DVD into your writable disc drive.**

   If you're copying a lot of files, insert a DVD into your DVD burner, as DVDs can store five times as much information as a CD. If you're giving away the disc to a friend, insert a blank CD, instead, as blank CDs cost less at the store.

3. **Decide how you want to use the disc.**

   Windows offers two options when creating the disc:

   • **Like a USB flash drive:** Choose this option when you intend for other PCs to read the disc. Windows 7 treats the disc much like a folder, letting you copy additional photos to the disc later. It's a good choice when you're backing up only a few pictures, because you can add more to the disc later.

   • **With a CD/DVD player:** Choose this option to create discs that play on CD and DVD players attached to TVs. After you write to the disc, it's sealed off so you can't write to it again. Don't choose this unless you plan to view the disc on a TV.

4. **Type a name for your backup disc and click Next.**

   Type today's date and the words **Photo Backup**, or something similarly descriptive. Windows 7 begins backing up all of that folder's photos to the disc.

5. **Click the Burn or Burn to Disc button again, if necessary.**

   If you selected With a CD/DVD Player in Step 3, click Burn to Disc to start copying your photos to the disc.

   If you didn't select any photos or folders in Step 1, Windows 7 opens an empty window showing the newly inserted disc's contents: nothing. Drag and drop the photos you want to burn into that window. Or, to copy them all, go back to the Pictures library and click Burn.

Don't have enough space on the CD or DVD to hold all your files? Unfortunately, Windows 7 isn't smart enough to tell you when to insert the second disc. Instead, it whines about not having enough room and doesn't burn *any* discs. In that case, head for Windows 7's much smarter backup program, which has the smarts to split your backup between several discs.

Printing Pictures

Windows 7's Photo Printing Wizard offers nearly as many options as the drugstore's photo counter, printing full-page glossies, wallet prints, and nearly anything in between.

The key to printing nice photos is buying nice (and expensive) photo paper and using a photo-quality printer. Ask to see printed samples before buying a printer and then buy that printer's recommended photo-quality paper.

Before printing your photos, feel free to crop and adjust their colors in a photo-editing program like Windows Live Photo Gallery.

Here's how to move photos from your screen to the printed page:

1. **Open Pictures from the Start menu and select the photos you'd like to print.**

   Want to print one photo? Then click it. To select more than one photo, hold down the Ctrl key as you click each one.

2. **Tell Windows 7 to print the selected photos.**

   You can tell Windows 7 to print your selection either of these ways:

   • Click the Print button from the folder's toolbar. You'll spot a handy Print button atop every folder in your Pictures library.

   • Right-click any of the selected photos and choose Print from the pop-up menu.

   No matter which method you choose, the Print Pictures window appears.

3. **Choose your printer, paper size, quality, paper type, photo layout, and the number of times to print each picture.**

   The Print Pictures window lets you tweak several settings. (If you don't tweak *anything,*

Windows 7 prints one copy of each photo across an expensive sheet of 8½-x-11-inch photo paper.)

- **Printer:** Windows 7 lists your default printer — your only printer, if you only have one — in the top-left drop-down list. If you own a second printer that you use only for photos, select that printer from the drop-down list.

- **Paper size:** Windows 7 lists different paper sizes in this drop-down list in case you'll be printing on something besides normal 8½-x-11-inch photo paper.

- **Quality:** Leave this at 600 x 600 dots per inch for most photo printers. If you're printing on a regular printer, switch to 300 x 300 dots per inch.

- **Paper Type:** Choose the type of paper you've placed in your printer, usually Photo Paper.

- **Layout:** On the Print Picture Windows' right edge, choose how Windows 7 should arrange the photos on the page. For example, you can print each photo to fill an entire page, print nine wallet photos, or print something in between. Each time you choose an option, the wizard displays a preview of the printed page.

- **Copies of each picture:** Choose anywhere from 1 to 99 copies of each picture.

- **Fit Picture to Frame:** Leave this check box selected so Windows 7 fills the paper with the photo. (This option may slightly crop your photo's edge a tad for a better fit.)

4. **Insert photo paper into your printer and click Print.**

   Follow the instructions for inserting your photo paper into your printer. It must face the correct direction and print on the correct side. Some paper requires a stiff paper backing sheet, as well.

   Click Print, and Windows 7 shuttles your photo off to the printer.

Most photo developers print digital photos with *much* better quality paper and ink than your own printer can accomplish. And with the cost of expensive printer paper and ink cartridges, photo developers often cost less than printing photos yourself. Check their pricing and ask the photo developer how you should submit your photos — by CD, memory card, or over the Internet.

Part II

Microsoft Office 2010

In this part...

*I*f you're already familiar with an earlier version of Microsoft Office, then staring at the bizarre appearance of today's Microsoft Office 2010 might feel foreign and alienating. However, after you get over your initial fear or hesitation about Microsoft Office 2010, you'll soon find that there's actually an elegance behind its seemingly chaotic appearance.

Since you can't really use Microsoft Office 2010 without knowing how to find the commands you need to make the program do what you want, this part of the book gently introduces you to the basics of using all of Office's programs. This part of the book also introduces you to the strange new Ribbon user interface and the Backstage View.

Before you know it, you'll be well on your way to understanding and feeling comfortable using Microsoft Office 2010. At that point, you can start using your favorite program and get something useful done. When you're ready to start using Office 2010's programs, flip to this part to find out everything you need to know on Word, Excel, Outlook, PowerPoint, and Access.

Chapter 9

Introducing Office 2010

• •

In This Chapter

▶ Starting an Office 2010 program

▶ Understanding the Microsoft Office Backstage View

▶ Using the Quick Access toolbar

▶ Figuring out the Ribbon

▶ Utilizing the Help window

▶ Previewing documents before printing

▶ Exiting from Office 2010

• •

*M*icrosoft Office 2010 consists of five core programs: Word, Excel, PowerPoint, Access, and Outlook. Each of these core programs specializes in manipulating different data. Word manipulates words, sentences, and paragraphs; Excel manipulates numbers; PowerPoint manipulates text and pictures to create a slide show; Access manipulates data, such as inventories; and Outlook manipulates personal information, such as e-mail addresses and phone numbers.

Although each Office 2010 program specializes in storing and manipulating different types of data, they all work in similar ways. First, you have to enter data into an Office 2010 program by typing on the keyboard or loading data from an existing file. Second, you have to tell Office 2010 how to manipulate your data, such as underlining, enlarging, coloring, or deleting it. Third, you have to save your data as a file.

To help you understand this three-step process of entering, manipulating, and saving data, Office 2010 offers similar commands among all its programs so you can quickly jump from Word to PowerPoint to Excel without having to learn entirely new commands to use each program. Even better, Office 2010 rearranges its numerous commands so finding the command you need is faster and easier than ever before. (If you think this implies that previous versions of Microsoft Office were clumsy and hard to use, you're right.)

If you're already familiar with computers and previous editions of Microsoft Office, you may want to browse through this chapter just to get acquainted with how Office 2010 rearranges common program commands. If you've never used a computer before or just don't feel comfortable using Microsoft Office, read this chapter first.

Starting an Office 2010 Program

The most straightforward way to load any Office 2010 program is to choose a program from the Start menu, and then create a new document or open an existing one. To do this, follow these steps:

1. **Click the Start button on the Windows taskbar.**

   A pop-up menu appears.

2. **Choose All Programs.**

   Another pop-up menu appears.

3. **Choose Microsoft Office.**

   A list of programs appears on the Start menu.

4. **Choose the Office 2010 program you want to use, such as Microsoft Word 2010 or Microsoft PowerPoint 2010.**

   Your chosen program appears on the screen. At this point, you can open an existing file.

Starting an Office 2010 program from the Start menu is most useful when you want to create a new document. If you just want to load an existing file, loading a Microsoft Office 2010 program and then loading that file is a clumsy two-step process. For a faster way to load a file and the Microsoft Office 2010 program that created it, follow these steps:

1. **Click the Start button on the Windows taskbar.**

   A pop-up menu appears.

2. **Choose Documents.**

   A dialog box appears.

3. **Double-click the file you want to open.**

   You may need to open a different folder or drive to find the file that you want.

Introducing the Microsoft Office Backstage View

One major change in Office 2010 is the Microsoft Office Backstage View, which replaces the traditional File menu in older versions of Office and the Office Button in Office 2007.

The Microsoft Office Backstage View appears in all Office 2010 programs and isolates common file commands on a single screen so you can see all your options at once, as shown in Figure 9-1:

- ✔ The left pane of the Backstage View lists common commands for creating, saving, or printing your file.

- ✔ The middle pane typically displays additional options you can choose for the command selected in the left pane.

- ✔ The right pane displays additional details about your file.

In Figure 9-1, the Info command is selected in the left pane, the middle pane displays three options, and the right pane displays detailed information about your document (and a preview of the document if it's available), such as how long you've been working on it and how many words it contains.

Figure 9-1: The new Microsoft Office Backstage View.

To use the Backstage View, follow these basic steps:

1. Click the File tab to display the Backstage View.

You can also open the Backstage View by pressing Alt+F and using either the keyboard or the mouse to choose additional commands.

2. Select a command in the left pane to view your options in the middle pane.

3. Select an option in the middle pane.

4. View the information (or select a command) in the right pane.

Sometimes when you select a command in the left pane (such as the Save command), you won't see any further options in the middle or right panes. Likewise, sometimes when you select an option in the middle pane, you won't see any additional information displayed in the right pane.

To exit the Backstage View, click the File tab again.

The File tab

The various commands available on the File tab include

- ✔ **Save:** Saves your file. If you haven't named your file yet, the Save command is equivalent to the Save As command.

- ✔ **Save As:** Saves the current file under a new name and/or in a different file format.

- ✔ **Open:** Loads an existing file.

- ✔ **Close:** Closes an open file but keeps the Office 2010 program running.

- ✔ **Recent:** Displays a list of files that you recently loaded.

- ✔ **New:** Creates a new file.

- ✔ **Print:** Prints the current file.

- ✔ **Share:** Sends a file as an e-mail attachment or fax along with saving the file in different formats (similar to the Save As command).

- ✔ **Options:** Displays various options for customizing the way each Office 2010 program behaves.

- ✔ **Exit:** Closes any open files and exits the Office 2010 program.

In Word, a file is called a *document.* In Excel, a file is called a *workbook.* In PowerPoint, a file is called a *presentation.* In Access, a file is called a *database.*

Creating a new file

Each time you create a new file, you have the option of choosing different types of templates that are already formatted and designed for specific purposes, such as a calendar, newsletter, sales report, or corporate slide show presentation.

To create a new file, follow these steps:

1. **Click the File tab.**

   The Backstage View appears.

2. **Click New.**

   A list of templates appears.

3. **Double-click the template you want to use.**

   Office 2010 creates a new file based on your chosen template. For some templates, you may need access to the Internet to download the templates from Microsoft's Web site.

Opening an existing file

When you load an Office 2010 program, you may want to edit a file that you created and modified earlier. To open an existing file, you need to tell Office 2010 the location and name of the file you want to open. Just follow these steps:

1. **Click the File tab.**

   The Backstage View appears.

2. **Click Open.**

   An Open dialog box appears.

3. (Optional) Click a folder, and then click Open to search for a file inside a folder. Repeat this step as many times as necessary.

4. Click the file you want to open, and then click Open.

Your chosen file appears, ready for editing.

Opening a recently used file

As a shortcut, Office 2010 keeps track of your most recently opened files and stores them in a list so you can find them again. If you need to open a file that you opened earlier, you may find it much faster by locating it through this list of recently opened files.

To open through the recently used file list, follow these steps:

1. **Click the File tab.**

   The Backstage View appears.

2. **Click Recent.**

   The list of recently opened files appears in the middle pane.

3. **Click a file.**

   Your chosen file appears.

The list of recently opened files changes each time you open a different file. If you want to keep a particular filename always displayed on this list, click the Pin icon that appears to the right of the filename.

Saving files

Saving a file stores all your data on a hard disk or other storage device (such as a USB flash drive). The first time you save a file, you need to specify three items:

- ✔ The drive and folder to store your file
- ✔ The name of your file
- ✔ The format to save your file

The drive and folder where you store your files are completely arbitrary. However, it's a good idea to store similar files in a folder with a descriptive name, such as *Tax Evasion Information for 2011* or *Extortion Letters to Grandma*. By default, Office 2010 stores all your files in the Documents folder.

The name of your file is also completely arbitrary, but it's also a good idea to give your file a descriptive name, such as *Latest Resume to Escape My Dead-End Job* or *Global Trade Presentation for World Domination Meeting on September 9, 2012.*

The format of your file defines how Office 2010 stores your data. The default file format is simply called Word Document, Excel Workbook, PowerPoint Presentation, or Access Database. Anyone using Office 2010 or Office 2007 can open these files.

Saving a file for Office 2010/2007

To save your files in the latest Office format, follow these steps:

1. **Click the File tab.**

   The Backstage View appears.

2. **Click Save.**

   If you have previously saved this file, you just need to complete Steps 1 and 2. If this is the first time you're saving the file, a Save As dialog box appears and you need to complete Steps 3, 4, and 5.

   For a quick way to save a file, click the Save icon that appears above the File tab or press Ctrl+S.

3. **Click in the File Name text box and type a descriptive name for your file.**

4. **(Optional) Click on a different folder or location to store your file.**

5. **Click Save.**

After you save a file once, you have to go through only Steps 1 and 2 again.

Saving a file for older versions of Microsoft Office

If you need to share files with people using older versions of Microsoft Office, you need to save your files in a different file format known as *97-2003,* such as *Word 97-2003 Document* or *PowerPoint 97-2003 Presentation.*

This special 97-2003 file format saves Office 2010 files so that previous versions of Microsoft Office 97/2000/XP/2003 can open and edit your files.

When you save files in the 97-2003 format, Microsoft Office 2010 saves your files with a three-letter file extension, like `.doc` or `.xls`. When you save files in the Office 2010 format, Microsoft Office 2010 saves your files with a four- or five-letter file extension, such as `.docx` or `.pptx`, as shown in Table 9-1.

Table 9-1	File Extension Names Used by Different Versions of Microsoft Office	
Program	*Microsoft Office 2010 File Extension*	*Microsoft Office 97-2003 File Extension*
Microsoft Word	`.docx`	`.doc`
Microsoft Excel	`.xlsx`	`.xls`
Microsoft PowerPoint	`.pptx`	`.ppt`
Microsoft Access	`.accdb`	`.mdb`

To save your Office 2010 files in the 97-2003 format, follow these steps:

1. **Click the File tab.**

   The Backstage View appears.

2. **Click Save & Send.**

   The middle pane displays different options.

3. **Click Change File Type under the File Types category.**

   A list of different formats appears.

4. **Click the 97-2003 format option, such as Word 97-2003 Document or Excel 97-2003 Workbook.**

   The Save As dialog box appears.

   If you want to share your file with different types of programs, you may need to choose a different file format, such as Rich Text Format or Text.

5. **(Optional) Click in the File Name text box and type a descriptive name for your file.**

6. **Click Save.**

Closing a file

When you're done editing a file, you need to close it. Closing a file simply removes the file from your screen but keeps your Office 2010 program running so you can edit or open another file. If you haven't saved your file, closing a file will prompt you to save your changes.

To close a file, follow these steps:

1. **Click the File tab.**

   The Backstage View appears.

2. **Click Close.**

   If you haven't saved your file, a dialog box appears asking whether you want to save your changes.

For a faster way to choose the Close command, press Ctrl+F4.

3. Click Yes to save your changes, No to discard any changes, or Cancel to keep your file open.

If you click either Yes or No, Office 2010 closes your file.

Using the Quick Access Toolbar

The Quick Access toolbar appears in the upper-left corner of the screen, displaying icons that represent commonly used commands such as Save, Undo, and Redo, as shown in Figure 9-2.

Quick Access toolbar

Figure 9-2: The Quick Access toolbar provides one-click access to the most commonly used commands.

Using the Quick Access icons

If you click the Save icon in the Quick Access toolbar, Office 2010 saves your current file. If you're saving a new file, a dialog box pops up, asking you to choose a name for your file.

The Redo icon reverses the last Undo command you chose. For example, if you delete a paragraph, Office 2010 makes that paragraph disappear. Then if you immediately click the Undo icon, the paragraph magically reappears. If you immediately click the Redo icon, the Redo command reverses the Undo command and deletes the paragraph once more.

The Undo icon is unique in that it offers two ways to use it. First, you can click the Undo icon to undo the last action you chose. Second, you can click the downward-pointing arrow that appears to the right of the Undo icon to display a list of one or more of your previous actions.

The most recent action you chose appears at the top of this list, the second most recent action appears second, and so on. To undo multiple commands, follow these steps:

1. **Click the downward-pointing arrow that appears to the right of the Undo icon in the Quick Access toolbar.**

2. **Move the mouse pointer to highlight one or more actions you want to undo.**

3. **Click the left mouse button.**

   Office 2010 undoes all the multiple actions you selected.

Using the Ribbon

With Office 2007, Microsoft abandoned the traditional pull-down menu bars and replaced them with the Ribbon, which organizes commands into categories called *contextual tabs.* Office 2010 uses the same Ribbon interface but with a slightly different look. If you're already familiar with Office 2007, you'll have no trouble learning Office 2010. If you've never used Office 2007, take some time to get acquainted with the Ribbon interface. At first it might seem strange, but over time, you'll see how handy it can be.

Each tab displays a different group of commands. For example, the Page Layout tab displays only those commands related to designing a page, and the Insert tab displays only those commands related to inserting items into a file, such as a page break or a picture, as shown in Figure 9-3. The Ribbon usually shows the Home tab when you start.

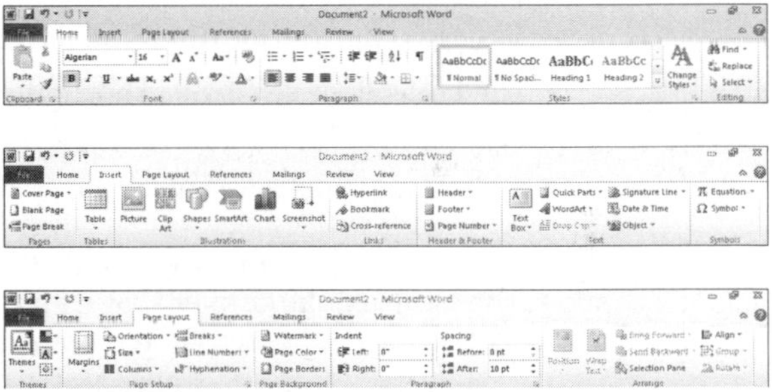

Figure 9-3: Each tab displays a different group of related commands.

Using the Ribbon is a two-step process. First, you must click the tab that contains the command you want. Second, you click the actual command.

Tabs act exactly like traditional pull-down menus. Whereas a pull-down menu simply displays a list of commands, tabs display a list of icons that represent different commands.

Identifying Ribbon icons

While some icons include descriptive text (such as Format Painter or Paste), most icons simply look like cryptic symbols from an alien language. To get additional help deciphering icons on the Ribbon, just point the mouse pointer over an icon and a short explanation appears, called a ScreenTip.

ScreenTips provide the following information:

- ✔ The official name of the command
- ✔ The equivalent keystroke shortcut you can use to run the command
- ✔ A short explanation of what the command does

To view the ScreenTip for any icon on the Ribbon, move the mouse pointer over that icon and wait a few seconds for the ScreenTip to appear.

Shortcut keystrokes let you choose a command from the keyboard without the hassle of clicking a tab and then clicking the icon buried inside that tab. Most shortcut keystrokes consist of two or three keys, such as Ctrl+P or Ctrl+Shift+C.

Displaying dialog boxes

On each tab, the Ribbon displays related commands in a group. For example, the Home tab groups the Cut, Copy, and Paste commands within the Clipboard group and the text alignment and line spacing commands within the Paragraph group.

Although you can choose the most commonly used commands directly from the Ribbon, Word often contains dozens of additional commands that don't appear on the Ribbon. To access these more obscure commands, you need to open a dialog box.

In the bottom-right corner of a group of icons on the Ribbon, you'll see the Show Dialog Box icon, which looks like an arrow pointing diagonally downward, as shown in Figure 9-4.

Figure 9-4: The Show Dialog Box appears in many grouped commands on the Ribbon.

Not every group of icons on the Ribbon displays the Show Dialog Box icon.

To open a dialog box that contains additional options, follow these steps:

1. **Click on a tab on the Ribbon, such as the Home or Page Layout tab.**

2. **Click on the Show Dialog Box icon in the bottom-right corner of a group such as the Font or Paragraph group found on the Home tab.**

   Office 2010 displays a dialog box.

3. **Choose any options in the dialog box, and then click OK or Cancel when you're done.**

Using Live Preview

With earlier versions of Office, you had to select data and then choose a command without knowing exactly how that command would affect the appearance of your data. If you didn't like the way a command changed your data, you had to choose the Undo command and start all over again.

To avoid this hassle of constant experimentation with different commands, Office 2010 offers a feature called *Live Preview*. Live Preview lets you move the mouse pointer over certain icons displayed in the Ribbon and then immediately see the changes displayed in your current file.

✔ If you like the way your data looks, go ahead and choose the command.

✔ If you don't like the way the data looks, just move the mouse away. Your data returns to its original appearance without forcing you to choose the Undo command.

To use Live Preview, follow these steps:

1. **Move the cursor (or click the mouse) on an object (text, picture, table, and so on) that you want to change.**

2. **Move the mouse pointer over any command.**

   Office 2010 shows you how your chosen object will look if you choose the command.

3. **Choose the command to change your object (or move the mouse pointer away from the command so you don't choose that command).**

In Word, Live Preview will not work if you display your document in Draft view.

Minimizing the Ribbon

Some people like the Ribbon displaying various icons at all times, but others find that it makes the screen appear too cluttered. In case you want to tuck the Ribbon out of sight (or display a Ribbon that is already tucked out of sight) so icons only appear when you click on a tab, choose one of the following methods as shown in Figure 9-5:

✔ Double-click on the current tab.

✔ Press Ctrl+F1.

✔ Click the Minimize Ribbon icon that appears on the far right next to the Help (Question Mark) icon.

Document2 - Microsoft Word

File   Home   Insert   Page Layout   References   Mailings   Review   View

Figure 9-5: The Ribbon can appear minimized.

To make the icons temporarily appear, click once on any tab. The moment you click away from the Ribbon, the Ribbon will hide its icons again.

Browsing the Help Window

Each Office 2010 program comes with its own help files that you can access at any time. To browse through the Help system, follow these steps:

1. **Choose one of the following to display the Help window, as shown in Figure 9-6:**

   • Click the Help icon.

   • Press F1.

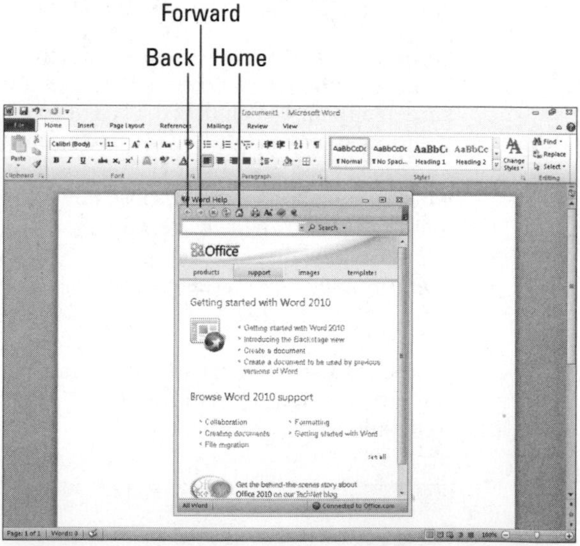

Forward

Back | Home

Figure 9-6: The Help window lets you search for answers to your questions.

2. **Click a topic.**

   The Help window displays a list of Help topics.

3. **Click a Help topic.**

   The Help window displays information about your chosen topic. You may need to click on multiple Help topics until you get the answer that you want.

4. **Click the Close box when you're done, to make the Help window go away.**

If you click the Back icon, you can view the previous text displayed in the Help window. If you click the Forward icon (after clicking the Back icon at least once), you can return forward to the text that you were looking at before you clicked the Back icon. If you click the Home icon, you can view the Help window's list of topics that appear every time you open the Help window.

Searching in the Help Window

Rather than browse through one or more subcategories to find help, you may want to search for help by typing in one or more keywords. Such keywords can identify a specific topic, such as *Printing* or *Editing charts*.

If you misspell a topic, the Help system may not understand what you want to find, so check your spelling.

To search the Help window by typing in a keyword or two, follow these steps:

1. **Choose one of the following methods to display the Help window (refer to Figure 9-6):**

   • Click the Help icon.

   • Press F1.

2. **Click in the Search list box and type one or more keywords, such as** Formatting **or** Aligning text.

   Type as few words as possible. So rather than type "I want to find help on printing," just type "Printing." Not only will this make it easier for you to search for help, but it will also keep Office 2010 from looking up extra words that have nothing to do with your topic such as "I want to find help on…"

3. **Click Search.**

   The Help window displays a list of topics.

4. **Click a Help topic.**

   The Help window displays information for your chosen topic. You may need to click on additional topics to get the answer you want.

5. **Click the Close box when you're done, to make the Help window go away.**

Previewing a Document before Printing

Before you print your document, you may want to preview how it will look so you don't waste paper printing something you can't use anyway. After you see that your pages will look perfect, then you can finally print out your document for everyone to read.

Defining page size and orientation

If you need to print your document on different sizes of paper, you may need to define the page size and paper orientation. By doing this, Word can accurately show you what your text may look like when printed on an 8.5" x 11" page compared with an 8.27" x 11.69" page.

To define the Page Size, follow these steps:

1. **Click the Page Layout tab.**

2. **Click the Size icon in the Page Setup group.**

   A pull-down menu appears.

3. **Click the page size you want.**

   Word displays your document based on the new page size.

Normally, Word assumes that you want to print in *portrait orientation,* where the height of the paper is larger than its width. However, you may want to print in *landscape orientation,* where the height of the paper is smaller than its width.

To define the orientation, follow these steps:

1. **Click the Page Layout tab.**

2. **Click the Orientation icon in the Page Setup group.**

   A pull-down menu appears.

3. **Click either Portrait or Landscape orientation.**

   Word displays your document based on the new paper orientation.

Using Print Preview

Print Preview lets you browse through your document so you can see how every page will look, including any headers and footers, cover pages, and pictures you may have added. To use Print Preview, follow these steps:

1. **Click the File tab.**

   The Backstage View appears.

2. **Click Print.**

   The Backstage View displays various print settings in the middle pane and a preview of your document in the right pane.

3. **(Optional) Click on the various options in the middle pane, such as choosing a printer to use or how many copies to print.**

4. **(Optional) Click Next Page/Previous Page or use the vertical scroll bar to browse through all the pages of your document.**

   If you drag the Magnifier slider in the bottom-right corner, you can zoom in or zoom out so you can examine the details of your document.

5. **Press Esc to return to your document, or click Print to start printing.**

   You can also start printing by just pressing Ctrl+P.

Exiting Office 2010

No matter how much you may love using Office 2010, eventually there will come a time when you need to exit an Office 2010 program and do something else with your life. To exit from any Office 2010 program, choose one of the following:

- ✔ Click the Close box in the upper-right corner of the Office 2007 window.
- ✔ Click the File tab, and then click Exit.
- ✔ Press Alt+F4.

If you try to close an Office 2010 program before saving your file, a dialog box pops up to give you a chance to save your file. If you don't save your file before exiting, you'll lose any changes you made to that file.

Chapter 10

Working with Word

● ●

In This Chapter

▶ Moving the cursor with the mouse and keyboard

▶ Viewing a document

▶ Finding and replacing text

▶ Checking spelling and grammar

▶ Playing with fonts, styles, and templates

▶ Creating new pages

● ●

*T*he whole purpose of Microsoft Word is to let you type in text and make it look pretty so you can print or send it for other people to read. So the first step in using Microsoft Word is finding how to enter text in a Word file, called a *document*.

In every document, Word displays a blinking cursor that points to where your text will appear if you type anything. To move the cursor, you can use the keyboard or the mouse.

Moving the Cursor with the Mouse

When you move the mouse, Word turns the mouse pointer into an I-beam pointer. If you move the mouse over an area where you cannot type any text, the mouse pointer turns back into the traditional arrow, pointing up to the left.

To move the cursor with the mouse, just point and click the left mouse button once. The blinking cursor appears where you clicked the mouse.

If you have a blank page or a blank area at the end of your document, you can move the cursor anywhere within this blank area by following these steps:

1. **Move the mouse pointer over any blank area past the end of a document.**

   Word defines the *end* of a document as the spot where no more text appears. To find the end of a document, press Ctrl+End.

   • *In a new document:* The end of the document is in the upper-left corner where the cursor appears.

   • *In a document with existing text:* The end of the document is the last area where text appears (including spaces or tabs).

   Notice that a Left, Left Indent, Center, or Right Justification icon appears to the right or bottom of the I-beam mouse pointer.

2. **Make sure that the correct justification icon appears next to the mouse pointer.**

For example, if you want to center-justify your text, make sure that the Center Justification icon appears at the bottom of the I-beam pointer.

Getting the Left, Center, or Right Justification icon to appear in Step 2 can be tricky. The Left Justification icon appears most of the time. If you move the mouse pointer slightly indented from the left margin of the page, the Left Indent icon appears. To make the Center Justification icon appear, move the mouse pointer to the center of the page. To make the Right Justification icon appear, move the mouse pointer to the right edge of the page.

3. Double-click the mouse pointer.

Word displays your cursor in the area you clicked. Any text you type now will appear justified according to the justification icon displayed in Step 3.

Moving the Cursor with the Keyboard

Moving the cursor with the mouse can be fast and easy. However, touch-typists often find that moving the cursor with the keyboard is more convenient and sometimes faster too. Table 10-1 lists different keystroke combinations you can use to move the cursor.

You can move the cursor with both the keyboard and the mouse.

Table 10-1	Keystroke Shortcuts for Moving the Cursor in Word
Keystroke	*What It Does*
↑	Moves the cursor up one line
↓	Moves the cursor down one line
→	Moves the cursor right one character
←	Moves the cursor left one character
Ctrl+↑	Moves the cursor up to the beginning of the preceding paragraph
Ctrl+↓	Moves the cursor down to the beginning of the next paragraph
Ctrl+→	Moves the cursor right one word
Ctrl+←	Moves the cursor left one word
Home	Moves the cursor to the beginning of the line
End	Moves the cursor to the end of the line
Ctrl+Home	Moves the cursor to the beginning of a document
Ctrl+End	Moves the cursor to the end of a document
Page Up	Moves the cursor up one screen
Page Down	Moves the cursor down one screen
Ctrl+Page Up	Moves the cursor to the top of the preceding page
Ctrl+Page Down	Moves the cursor to the top of the next page

Viewing a Document

Word can display your document in one of five views, which can help you better understand the layout, margins, and page breaks in your document:

- ✔ **Print Layout:** Displays page breaks as thick, dark horizontal bars so you can clearly see where a page ends and begins. (This is the default view.)

- ✔ **Full Screen Reading:** Displays pages side by side so you see how adjacent pages appear next to each other.

- ✔ **Web Layout:** Displays your document exactly as it would appear if you saved it as a Web page.

- ✔ **Outline:** Displays your document as outline headings and subheadings.

- ✔ **Draft:** Displays the document without top or bottom page margins where page breaks appear as dotted lines.

Finding and Replacing Text

To help you find text, Word offers a handy Find feature. Not only can this Find feature search for a word or phrase, but it also offers a Replace option so you can make Word find certain words and automatically replace them with other words.

Using the Find command

The Find command can search for a single character, word, or a group of words. To make searching faster, you can either search an entire document or just a specific part of a document. To make searching a document more flexible, Word lets you search for specific words or phrases, headings, or pages.

Searching for text

To search for words or phrases by using the Find command, follow these steps:

1. **Click the Home tab.**

2. **Click the Find icon in the Editing group.**

   The Navigation Pane appears in the left side of the screen.

   If you click the downward-pointing arrow to the right of the Find icon, a menu appears that lets you choose the Find or Go To command.

3. **Click in the Search Document text box, type a word or phrase to find, and press Enter.**

   The Navigation Pane lists all matching text.

   As you type, Word displays all matching text. So if you start typing **he**, Word will find all text that matches "he," such as "hello," "helicopter," or "help."

4. **Click on any of the text displayed in the Navigation Pane.**

   Word highlights your chosen text in your document.

5. **Click on the X icon that appears in the Search Document text box in the Navigation pane.**

   Word clears the text you typed in Step 3.

Using the Find and Replace command

Rather than just find a word or phrase, you may want to find that text and replace it with something else. To use the Find and Replace command, follow these steps:

1. **Click the Home tab.**

2. **Click the Replace icon in the Editing group. (You can also press Ctrl+H.)**

   The Find and Replace dialog box appears, as shown in Figure 10-1.

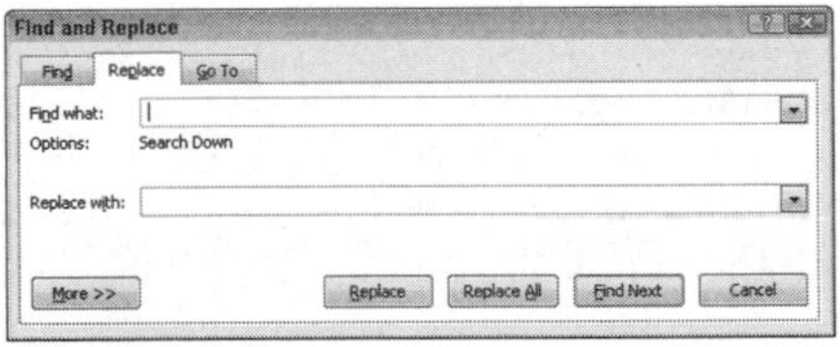

Figure 10-1: The Find and Replace dialog box provides options for replacing text.

3. **Click in the Find What text box and type a word or phrase to find.**

4. **Click in the Replace With text box and type a word or phrase to replace the text you typed in Step 3.**

5. **(Optional) Click the More button and choose any additional options.**

6. **Click one of the following buttons:**

   - *Replace All:* Searches and replaces text throughout the entire document

   - *Replace:* Replaces the currently highlighted text

   - *Find Next:* Searches from the current cursor location to the end of the document

7. **Click Find Next to search for additional occurrences of the text you typed in Step 3.**

8. **Click Cancel to make the Find and Replace dialog box disappear.**

Checking Your Spelling

As you type, Word tries to correct your spelling automatically. (Try it! Type **tjhe**, and Word will automatically change it to *the* in the blink of an eye.) If you type something that Word doesn't recognize, it underlines it with a red squiggly line.

Just because Word underlines a word doesn't necessarily mean that the word is spelled wrong. It could be a proper name, a foreign word, or just a word that Word isn't smart enough to recognize.

To correct any words that Word underlines with a red squiggly line, follow these steps:

1. **Right-click any word underlined with a red squiggly line.**

   A pop-up menu appears.

2. **Choose one of the following:**

   - *The word you want:* Click the correct spelling of the word that appears in bold in the pop-up menu.

   - *Ignore:* This tells Word to ignore this word but flag this same word anywhere else in your document.

   - *Ignore All:* This tells Word to ignore this word throughout your document.

   - *Add to Dictionary:* This tells Word to remember this word and never flag it again as a misspelled word.

Changing the Font

The most common way to format text is to change the font. The font defines the uniform style and appearance of letters such as Baskerville, Courier, Old English, or **STENCIL**.

To change the font, follow these steps:

1. **Click the Home tab.**

2. **Select the text you want to change.**

3. **Click the Font list box.**

   A list of available fonts on your computer appears.

4. **Move the mouse pointer over each font.**

   Word temporarily changes your selected text (from Step 2) so you can see how the currently highlighted font will look.

5. **Click the font you want to use.**

   Word changes your text to appear in your chosen font.

As a general rule, try not to use more than three fonts in a document. If you use too many fonts, the overall appearance can be annoying and DISTRACTING.

Not all computers have the same lists of fonts, so if you plan on sharing documents with others, stick with common fonts that everybody's computer can display.

Changing the Font Size

The *font* changes the appearance of text, but the *font size* defines how big (or small) the text may look. To change the font size, you have two choices:

- ✔ Select a numeric size from the Font Size list box.
- ✔ Choose the Grow Font/Shrink Font commands.

You can use both methods to change the font size of text. For example, you may use the Font Size list box to choose an approximate size for your text, and then use the Grow Font/Shrink Font commands to fine-tune the font size.

To change the font size, follow these steps:

1. **Click the Home tab.**

2. **Select the text you want to change.**

3. **Choose one of the following:**

   - Click the Font Size list box and then click a number, such as 12 or 24.

   - Click the Grow Font or Shrink Font icon.

Changing the Text Style

The text style defines the appearance of text in one or more of the following ways:

- **Bold:** Press Ctrl+B.

- *Italic:* Press Ctrl+I.

- <u>Underline</u>: Press Ctrl+U.

- ~~Strikethrough~~: This formatting draws a line through text.

- Subscript: Use this to create text that falls below the text line, as in the 2 in H_2O.

- Superscript: Use this to create text that sits higher than the top of the text line, as in the 2 in $E = mc^2$.

To change the style of text, follow these steps:

1. **Click the Home tab.**

2. **Select the text you want to change.**

3. **Click a Style icon, such as Bold or Underline.**

4. **Repeat Step 3 for each additional style you want to apply to your text (such as *italic* and <u>underlining</u>).**

If you select any style change without selecting any text, Word applies your style changes to any new text you type from the cursor's current position.

Changing Colors

Color can emphasize text. There are two ways to use color:

- ✔ Change the color of the text (Font color).
- ✔ Highlight the text with a different color (Text Highlight color).

Changing the color of text

When you change the color of text, you're physically displaying a different color for each letter. Normally, Word displays text in black, but you can change the color to anything you want, such as bright red or dark green.

If you choose a light color for your text, it may be hard to read against a white background.

To change the color of text, follow these steps:

1. **Click the Home tab.**

2. **Select the text you want to color.**

3. **Click the downward-pointing arrow to the right of the Font Color icon.**

A color palette appears.

4. **Click a color.**

Word displays your selected text (from Step 2) in your chosen color.

After you choose a color, that color appears directly on the Font Color icon. Now you can select text and click directly on the Font Color icon (not the downward-pointing arrow) to color your text.

Highlighting text with color

Highlighting text mimics coloring chunks of text with a highlighting marker that students often use to emphasize passages in a book. To highlight text, follow these steps:

1. **Click the Home tab.**

2. **Select the text you want to highlight.**

3. **Click the downward-pointing arrow to the right of the Text Highlight Color icon.**

A color palette appears.

4. **Click a color.**

Word highlights your selected text (from Step 2) in your chosen color.

5. **Press Esc (or click the Text Highlight Color icon again) to turn off the Text Highlight Color command.**

To remove a highlight, select the text and choose the same color again.

If no text is selected and the Text Highlight Color currently displays a color you want to use (such as yellow), you can click the Text Highlight Color icon (not its downward-pointing arrow). This turns the mouse pointer into a marker icon. Now you can select and highlight text in one step.

Using Styles

As an alternative to choosing fonts, font sizes, and text styles (like bold) individually, Word offers several predefined formatting styles. To apply a style to your text, follow these steps:

1. **Click the Home tab.**

2. **Select the text that you want to format.**

3. **Click the up/down arrows of the Styles scroll bar to scroll through the different styles available. Or click the More button to display a pull-down menu of all the Quick Formatting styles, as shown in Figure 10-2.**

4. **Move the mouse pointer over a style.**

   Word displays what your text will look like if you choose this style.

5. **Click the style you want to use, such as Heading 1, Title, or Quote.**

   Word formats your text.

Figure 10-2: Clicking the More button displays a menu of all available styles.

Using Templates

In case you need to format an entire document a certain way, you may want to use templates instead. *Templates* act like preformatted documents. Word comes with
several templates, but Microsoft offers several through its Web site as well.

To create a new document from a template, follow these steps:

1. Click the File tab and then choose New.

An Available Templates window appears, as shown in Figure 10-3.

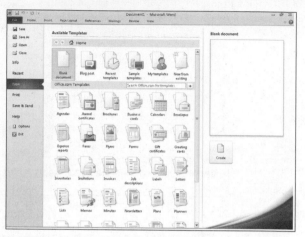

Figure 10-3: Templates let you create a new document based on the formatting of an existing file.

> 2. **Double-click on a template.**
>
>   Word creates a blank document with "dummy" text to show you how the formatting looks.
>
> 3. **Type new text into your newly created document.**
>
>
>
>   You may need to be connected to the Internet to download some of the available templates.

Removing Formatting from Text

After you format text, you can always remove that formatting. The simplest way to do this is to apply the same formatting you want to remove. For example, if you underline text, you can remove the underlining by highlighting all the underlined text and choosing the underline command (by pressing Ctrl+U or by clicking the Underline icon).

If you want to remove multiple formatting from text, you could remove each formatting style one by one, but it's much easier just to use the Clear Formatting command instead, which removes all formatting on text no matter how much formatting there may be.

To use the Clear Formatting command, follow these steps:

1. **Click the Home tab.**

2. **Select the text that contains the formatting you want to remove.**

3. **Click the Clear Formatting icon, as shown in Figure 10-4.**

   Word removes all formatting from your selected text.

Figure 10-4: The Clear Formatting icon removes all text formatting.

The Clear Formatting command will not remove any highlighting you may have applied over text.

Inserting New Pages

Word automatically adds new pages to your document as you write. However, Word also gives you the option of adding a new page anywhere in your document, such as in the middle or the beginning.

To insert a new, blank page in your document, follow these steps:

1. **Click the Insert tab.**
2. **Move the cursor where you want to insert the new page.**
3. **Click the Blank Page icon in the Pages group.**

   Word adds a blank page to your document where the cursor appears. So if you put the cursor between two sentences and insert a blank page, the first sentence will appear on one page, a blank page will appear next, and the second sentence will appear after the blank page.

You don't need to add a page to the end of a document. Just move the cursor to the end of your document (Ctrl+End), start typing, and Word automatically adds new pages at the end of your document.

Inserting Page Breaks

Rather than insert a new page, you may want to break text on an existing page into two pages. To insert a page break in your document, follow these steps:

1. **Move the cursor where you want to break your document into two pages.**

2. **Click the Insert tab.**

3. **Click the Page Break icon in the Pages group.**

   Word breaks your document into two pages.

To delete a page break, move the cursor to the top of the page directly following the page break you want to delete. Then press Backspace.

As an alternative to following Steps 2 and 3 in the preceding step list, you can just press Ctrl+Enter to create a page break at the cursor's current location.

Chapter 11

Playing the Numbers with Excel

. . . .

In This Chapter

▶ Getting familiar with spreadsheets

▶ Typing and formatting data

▶ Editing a spreadsheet

▶ Working with formulas

▶ Utilizing functions

▶ Going visual with charts

. . . .

*E*veryone needs to perform simple math. Businesses need to keep track of sales and profits, and individuals need to keep track of budgets. In the old days, people not only had to write down numbers on paper, but they also had to do all their calculations by hand (or with the aid of a calculator).

That's why people use Excel. Instead of writing numbers on paper, they can type numbers on the computer. Instead of adding or subtracting columns or rows of numbers by hand, Excel can do it for you automatically. Basically, Excel makes it easy to type and modify numbers and then calculate new results accurately and quickly.

Besides calculating numbers, spreadsheets can also store lists of data organized in rows and columns.

Understanding Spreadsheets

Excel organizes numbers in rows and columns. An entire page of rows and columns is called a *spreadsheet* or a *worksheet.* (A collection of one or more worksheets is stored in a file called a *workbook.*) Each row is identified by a number such as 1 or 249; and each column is identified by letters, such as A, G, or BF. The intersection of each row and column defines a *cell,* which contains one of three items:

- ✔ Numbers
- ✔ Text (labels)
- ✔ Formulas

Numbers provide the data, and *formulas* calculate that data to produce a useful result, such as adding sales results for the week. Of course, just displaying numbers on the screen may be confusing if you don't know what those numbers mean, so labels simply identify what numbers represent. Figure 11-1 shows the parts of a typical spreadsheet.

Formulas usually appear as numbers, so at first glance, it may be difficult to tell the difference between ordinary numbers and numbers that represent a calculation by a formula.

The strength of spreadsheets comes by playing "What-if?" games with your data, such as "What if I gave myself a $20-per-hour raise and cut everyone else's salary by 25%? How much money would that save the company every month?" Because spread-sheets can rapidly calculate new results, you can experiment with different numbers to see how they create different answers.

Labels

Formulas   Numbers

Figure 11-1: The parts of a typical spreadsheet.

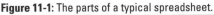

Storing Stuff in a Spreadsheet

Every cell can contain a number, a label, or a for-mula. To type anything into a spreadsheet, you must first select or click in the cell (or cells) and then type a number or text.

Typing data into a single cell

To type data in a single cell, follow these steps:

1. **Choose one of the following to select a single cell:**

   • Click a cell.

   • Press the up/down/right/left arrow keys to highlight a cell.

2. **Type a number (such as 34.29 or 198), a label (such as Tax Returns), or a formula.**

Typing data in multiple cells

After you type data in a cell, you can press one of the following four keystrokes to select a different cell:

✔ **Enter:** Selects the cell below in the same column

✔ **Tab:** Selects the cell to the right in the same row

✔ **Shift+Enter:** Selects the cell above in the same column

✔ **Shift+Tab:** Selects the cell to the left in the same row

If you type data in cell A1 and press Enter, Excel selects the next cell below, which is A2. If you type data in A2 and press Tab, Excel selects the cell to the right, which is B2.

However, what if you want to type data in a cell such as A1 and then have Excel select the next cell to the right (B1)? Or what if you want to type data in cells A1 and A2 but then jump back to type additional data in cells B1 and B2?

To make this easy, Excel lets you select a range of cells, which essentially tells Excel, "See all the cells I just highlighted? I only want to type data in those cells." After you select multiple cells, you can type data and press Enter. Excel selects the next cell down in that same column. When Excel reaches the last cell in the column, it selects the top cell of the column to the right.

To select multiple cells for typing data in, follow these steps:

1. **Highlight multiple cells by choosing one of the following:**

   • Move the mouse pointer over a cell, hold down the left mouse button, and drag (move) the mouse to highlight multiple cells. Release the left mouse button when you've selected enough cells.

   • Hold down the Shift key and press the up/down/right/left arrow keys to high-light multiple cells. Release the Shift key when you've selected enough cells.

   Excel selects the cell that appears in the upper-left corner of your selected cells.

2. **Type a number, label, or formula.**

3. **Press Enter.**

   Excel selects the cell directly below the preceding cell. If the preceding cell appeared at the bottom of the selected column, Excel highlights the top cell in the column that appears to the right.

4. **Repeat Steps 2 and 3 until you fill your selected cells with data.**

5. **Click outside the selected cells or press an arrow key to tell Excel not to select the cells any more.**

Navigating a Spreadsheet

If you have a large spreadsheet, chances are good that information may be hidden by the limitations of your computer screen. To help you view and select cells in different parts of your spreadsheet, Excel offers various ways to navigate a spreadsheet by using the mouse and keyboard.

Using the mouse to move around in a spreadsheet

To navigate a spreadsheet with the mouse, you can click the scroll bars or use the scroll wheel, on your mouse, if you have one. To use the scroll bars, you have three choices:

✔ **Click the up/down or right/left arrows on the horizontal or vertical scroll bars.**

This moves the spreadsheet one row (up or down) or column (right or left) at a time.

✔ **Drag the scroll box of a scroll bar.**

✔ **Click the scroll area (any area to the left/right or above/below the scroll box on the scroll bar).**

This moves the spreadsheet one screen left/right or up/down.

If your mouse has a scroll wheel, you can use this wheel to move through a spreadsheet by two methods:

- ✔ Roll the mouse's scroll wheel up or down to scroll your spreadsheet up or down.

- ✔ Press the scroll wheel to display a four-way pointing arrow, and then move the mouse up, down, right, or left. (When you're done, click the scroll wheel again.)

Using the keyboard to move around a spreadsheet

Using the mouse can be faster to jump from one place in a spreadsheet to another, but sometimes using the mouse can be frustrating, trying to line it up just right. For that reason, you can also use the keyboard to move around a spreadsheet. Some of the common ways to move around a spreadsheet are shown in Table 11-1.

Table 11-1   Using the Keyboard to Navigate a Spreadsheet

Pressing This	Does This
Up arrow (↑)	Moves up one row
Down arrow (↓)	Moves down one row
Left arrow (←)	Moves left one column
Right arrow (→)	Moves right one column

(continued)

Table 11-1 *(continued)*

Pressing This	Does This
Ctrl+↑	Jumps up to the top of a column that contains data
Ctrl+↓	Jumps down to the bottom of a column that contains data
Ctrl+←	Jumps to the left of a row that contains data
Ctrl+→	Jumps to the right of a row that contains data
Page Up	Moves up one screen
Page Down	Moves down one screen
Ctrl+Page Up	Displays the previous worksheet
Ctrl+Page Down	Displays the next worksheet
Home	Moves to the A column of the current row
Ctrl+Home	Moves to the A1 cell
Ctrl+End	Moves to the bottom-right cell of your spreadsheet

If you know the specific cell you want to move to, you can jump to that cell by using the Go To command. To use the Go To command, follow these steps:

1. Click the Home tab.

2. **Click the Find & Select icon in the Editing group.**

   A pull-down menu appears.

3. **Click Go To.**

   The Go To dialog box appears.

   You can also choose the Go To command by pressing Ctrl+G.

4. **Click in the Reference text box and type the cell you want to move to, such as C13 or F4.**

5. **Click OK.**

   Excel highlights the cell you typed in Step 4.

Editing a Spreadsheet

The two ways to edit a spreadsheet are

- ✓ Edit the data itself, such as the labels, numbers, and formulas that make up a spreadsheet.

- ✓ Edit the physical layout of the spreadsheet, such as adding or deleting rows and columns, or widening or shrinking the width or height of rows and columns.

Editing data in a cell

To edit data in a single cell, follow these steps:

1. **Double-click the cell that contains the data you want to edit.**

   Excel displays a cursor in your selected cell.

2. **Edit your data by using the Backspace or Delete key, or by typing new data.**

If you click a cell, Excel displays the contents of that cell in the Formula bar. You can click and edit data directly in the Formula bar, which can be more convenient for editing large amounts of data such as a formula.

Changing the size of rows and columns with the mouse

Using the mouse can be a quick way to modify the sizes of rows and columns. To change the height of a row or the width of a column, follow these steps:

1. **Move the mouse pointer over the bottom line of a row heading, such as the 2 or 18 heading. (Or move the mouse pointer over the right line of the column heading, such as A or D.)**

   The mouse pointer turns into a two-way pointing arrow.

2. **Hold down the left mouse button and drag (move) the mouse.**

   Excel resizes your row or column.

3. **Release the left mouse button when you're happy with the size of your row or column.**

Typing the size of rows and columns

If you need to resize a row or column to a precise value, it's easier to type a specific value into the

Row Height or Column Width dialog box instead. To type a value into a Row Height or Column Width dialog box, follow these steps:

1. **Click the Home tab.**

2. **Click the row or column heading that you want to resize.**

   Excel highlights your entire row or column.

3. **Click the Format icon that appears in the Cells group.**

   A pull-down menu appears.

4. **Click Height (if you selected a row) or Width (if you selected a column).**

   The Row Height or Column Width dialog box appears.

5. **Type a value and then click OK.**

   Excel resizes your row or column.

 Excel measures column width in characters. (A cell defined as 1 character width can display a single letter or number.) Excel measures row height by points where 1 point equals 1/72 inch.

Adding and deleting rows and columns

After you type in labels, numbers, and formulas, you may suddenly realize that you need to add or delete extra rows or columns. To add a row or column, follow these steps:

1. Click the Home tab.

2. Click the row or column heading where you want to add another row or column.

   Excel highlights the entire row or column.

3. Click the Insert icon in the Cells group.

   Inserting a row adds a new row above the selected row. Inserting a column adds a new column to the left of the selected column.

To delete a row or column, follow these steps:

1. Click the Home tab.

2. Click the row or column heading that you want to delete.

3. Click the Delete icon in the Cells group.

Deleting a row or column deletes any data stored in that row or column.

Adding sheets

For greater flexibility, Excel lets you create individual spreadsheets that you can save in a single workbook (file). When you load Excel, it automatically provides you with three sheets, but you can add more if you need them.

To add a new sheet, choose one of the following:

✔ Click the Insert Worksheet icon that appears to the right of your existing tabs (or press Shift+F11).

✔ **Click the Home tab, click the downward-pointing arrow next to the Insert icon in the Cells group, and then choose Insert Sheet, as shown in Figure 11-2.**

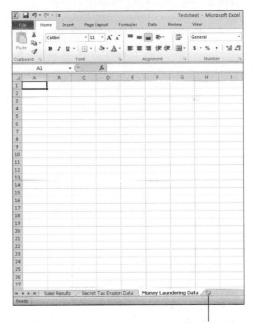

Insert Worksheet icon

Figure 11-2: Excel displays the names of individual sheets as tabs.

Renaming sheets

By default, Excel gives each sheet a generic name such as Sheet1. To give your sheets a more descriptive name, follow these steps:

1. Choose one of the following:

- *Double-click the sheet tab that you want to rename.*

  Excel highlights the entire sheet name.

- *Click the sheet tab you want to rename, click the Home tab, click the Format icon in the Cells group, and choose Rename Sheet.*

- *Right-click the sheet tab you want to rename; when a pop-up menu appears, choose Rename.*

2. Type a new name for your sheet and press Enter when you're done.

Your new name appears on the sheet tab.

Deleting a sheet

Using multiple sheets may be handy, but you may want to delete a sheet if you don't need it.

If you delete a sheet, you also delete all the data stored on that sheet.

To delete a sheet, follow these steps:

1. Click on the sheet that you want to delete.

2. Choose one of the following:

> • *Right-click the tab of the sheet you want to delete. When a pop-up menu appears, click Delete.*
>
> • *Click the Home tab, click the downward-pointing arrow that appears to the right of the Delete icon in the Cells group, and choose Delete Sheet.*

If your sheet is empty, Excel deletes the sheet right away. If your sheet contains data, a dialog box appears to warn you that you'll lose any data stored on that sheet.

3. Click Delete.

Excel deletes your sheet along with any data on it.

Creating a Formula

Formulas consist of three crucial bits of information:

- ✔ An equal sign (=)
- ✔ One or more cell references
- ✔ The type of calculation to do on the data (addition, subtraction, and so on)

A *cell reference* is simply the unique row and column heading that identifies a single cell, such as A4 or D9. The four common calculations that a formula can use are addition (+), subtraction (–), multiplication (*), and division (/).

A simple formula uses a single mathematical operator and two cell references such as:

    =A4+C7

This formula consists of three parts:

- **The = sign:** This identifies your formula. If you type just **A4+C7** into a cell, Excel treats it as ordinary text.

- **Two cell references:** In this example, A4 and C7.

- **The addition (+) mathematical operator.**

To type a formula in a cell, follow these steps:

1. **Click in the cell where you want to store the formula.**

   You can also select a cell by pressing the arrow keys.

   Excel highlights your selected cell.

2. **Type the equal sign (=).**

   This tells Excel that you are creating a formula.

3. **Type your formula that includes one or more cell references that identify cells that contain data, such as A4 or E8.**

   For example, if you want to add the numbers stored in cells A4 and E8, you would type =A4+E8.

4. **Press Enter.**

Typing cell references can get cumbersome because you have to match the row and column headings of a cell correctly. As a faster alternative, you can use the mouse to click any cell that contains data; then Excel types that cell reference into your formula automatically.

To use the mouse to click cell references when creating a formula, follow these steps:

1. **Click in the cell where you want to store the formula. (You can also select the cell by pressing the arrow keys.)**

   Excel highlights your selected cell.

2. **Type the equal sign (=).**

   This tells Excel that anything you type after the equal sign is part of your formula.

3. **Type any mathematical operators and click any cells that contain data, such as A4 or E8.**

   If you want to create the formula =A4+E8, you would do the following:

   a. Type =.

      This tells Excel that you're creating a formula.

   b. Click cell A4.

      Excel types the A4 cell reference in your formula automatically.

   c. Type +.

   d. Click cell E8.

      Excel types in the E8 cell reference in your formula automatically.

4. **Press Enter.**

After you finish creating a formula, you can type data into the cell references used in your formula to calculate a new result.

Organizing formulas with parentheses

Formulas can be as simple as a single mathematical operator such as =D3*E4. However, you can also use multiple mathematical operators, such as

=A4+A5*C7/F4+D9

There are two problems with using multiple mathematical operators. First, they make a formula harder to read and understand. Second, Excel calculates mathematical operators from left to right, based on precedence, which means a formula may calculate results differently than you intended.

Precedence tells Excel which mathematical operators to calculate first, as listed in Table 11-2. For example, Excel calculates multiplication before it calculates addition. If you had a formula like

=A3+A4*B4+B5

Excel first multiplies A4*B4 and then adds this result to A3 and B5.

Table 11-2	Operator Precedence in Excel
Mathematical Operator	*Description*
: (colon) (single space) , (comma)	Reference operators
–	Negation

Mathematical Operator	Description
%	Percent
^	Exponentiation
* /	Multiplication and division
+ −	Addition and subtraction
&	Text concatenation
= < > <= >= <>	Comparison

Typing parentheses around cell references and mathematical operators not only organizes your formulas, but also tells Excel specifically how you want to calculate a formula. In the example =A3+A4*B4+B5, Excel multiplies A4 and B4 first. If you want Excel to first add A3 and A4, then add B4 and B5, and finally multiply the two results together, you have to use parentheses, like this:

=(A3+A4)*(B4+B5)

Copying formulas

In many spreadsheets, you may need to create similar formulas that use different data. For example, you may have a spreadsheet that needs to add the same number of cells in adjacent columns.

You could type nearly identical formulas in multiple cells, but that's tedious and error-prone. For a faster way, you can copy a formula and paste it in another cell; then Excel automatically changes the cell references.

To copy and paste a formula so that each formula changes cell references automatically, follow these steps:

1. **Select the cell that contains the formula you want to copy.**

2. **Press Ctrl+C (or click the Copy icon under the Home tab).**

   Excel displays a dotted line around your selected cell.

3. **Select the cell (or cells) where you want to paste your formula.**

   If you select multiple cells, Excel pastes a copy of your formula in each of those cells.

4. **Press Ctrl+V (or click the Paste icon under the Home tab).**

   Excel pastes your formula and automatically changes the cell references.

5. **Press Esc or double-click away from the cell with the dotted line to make the dotted line go away.**

Using Functions

Creating simple formulas is easy, but creating complex formulas is hard. To make complex formulas easier to create, Excel comes with prebuilt formulas called functions. Here are some of the many functions available:

 AVERAGE: Calculates the average value of numbers stored in two or more cells.

- **COUNT:** Counts how many cells contain a number instead of a label (text).

- **MAX:** Finds the largest number stored in two or more cells.

- **MIN:** Finds the smallest number stored in two or more cells.

- **ROUND:** Rounds a decimal number to a specific number of digits.

- **SQRT:** Calculates the square root of a number.

- **SUM:** Adds the values stored in two or more cells.

Excel literally provides hundreds of functions that you can use by themselves or as part of your own formulas. A function typically uses one or more cell references:

- **Single cell references,** such as =ROUND(C4,2), which rounds the number found in cell C4 to two decimal places

- *Contiguous* **(adjacent) cell ranges,** such as =SUM(A4:A9), which adds all the numbers found in cells A4, A5, A6, A7, A8, and A9

- **Noncontiguous cell ranges,** such as =SUM(A4,B7,C11), which adds all the numbers found in cells A4, B7, and C11

To use a function, follow these steps:

1. **Click in the cell where you want to create a formula using a function.**

2. **Click the Formulas tab.**

3. **Click one of the following function icons in the Function Library group:**

   - *Financial:* Calculates business-related equations, such as the amount of interest earned over a specified time period

   - *Logical:* Provides logical operators to manipulate True and False (also known as *Boolean*) values

   - *Text:* Searches and manipulates text

   - *Date & Time:* Provides date and time information

   - *Lookup & Reference:* Provides information about cells, such as their row headings

   - *Math & Trig:* Offers mathematical equations

   - *More Functions:* Provides access to statistical and engineering functions

4. **Click a function category, such as Financial or Math & Trig.**

   A pull-down menu appears.

5. **Click a function.**

   The Function Arguments dialog box appears.

6. **Click the cell references you want to use.**

7. **Repeat Step 6 as many times as necessary.**

8. **Click OK.**

   Excel displays the calculation of your function in the cell you selected in Step 1.

Using the AutoSum command

One of the most useful and commonly used command is the AutoSum command. The *AutoSum command* uses the SUM function to add two or more cell references without making you type those cell references yourself. The most common use for the AutoSum function is to add a column or row of numbers.

To add a column or row of numbers with the AutoSum function, follow these steps:

1. **Create a column or row of numbers that you want to add.**

2. **Click at the bottom of the column or the right of the row.**

3. **Click the Formulas tab.**

4. **Click the AutoSum icon in the Function Library group.**

   Excel automatically creates a SUM function in the cell you chose in Step 2 and highlights all the cells where it will retrieve data to add. (If you accidentally click the downward-pointing arrow under the AutoSum icon, a pull-down menu appears. Just choose Sum.)

5. **Press Enter.**

   Excel automatically sums all the cell references.

The AutoSum icon also appears on the Home tab in the Editing group.

Using recently used functions

Digging through all the different function library menus can be cumbersome, so Excel tries to make your life easier by creating a special Recently Used list that contains (what else?) a list of the functions you've used most often. From this menu, you can see just a list of your favorite functions and ignore the other hundred functions that you may never need in a million years.

To use the list of recently used functions, follow these steps:

1. **Click the cell where you want to store a function.**

2. **Click the Formulas tab.**

3. **Click the Recently Used icon in the Function Library group.**

   A pull-down menu appears.

4. **Choose a function.**

Editing a Formula

After you create a formula, you can always edit it later. You can edit a formula in two places:

- ✔ In the Formula bar
- ✔ In the cell itself

To edit a formula in the Formula bar, follow these steps:

1. **Select the cell that contains the formula you want to edit.**

   Excel displays the formula in the Formula bar.

2. **Click in the Formula bar and edit your formula by using the Backspace and Delete keys.**

To edit a formula in the cell itself, follow these steps:

1. **Double-click in the cell that contains the formula you want to edit.**

   Excel displays a cursor in the cell you selected.

2. **Edit your formula by using the Backspace and Delete keys.**

Because formulas display their calculations in a cell, it can be hard to tell the difference between cells that contain numbers and cells that contain formulas. To make formulas visible, press Ctrl+` (an accent grave character, which appears on the same key as the ~ symbol).

Understanding the Parts of a Chart

To create charts that clarify your data (rather than confuse you even more), you need to understand the parts of a chart and their purpose, as shown in Figure 11-3:

- ✔ **Data Series:** The numeric data that Excel uses to create the chart

- ✔ **X-axis:** Defines the width of a chart

✔ **Y-axis:** Defines the height of a chart

✔ **Legend:** Provides text to explain what each visual part of a chart means

✔ **Chart Title:** Explains the purpose of the entire chart

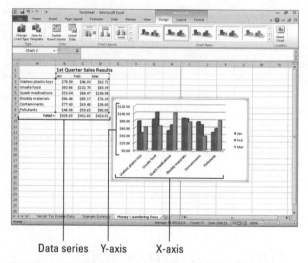

Data series   Y-axis   X-axis

Figure 11-3: Each part of a typical Excel chart displays information about your data.

Charts typically use two data series to create a chart. For example, one data series may be sales made that month, while a second data series may be the names of each salesperson.

The X-axis of such a chart would list the names of different products while the Y-axis would list a range of numbers that represent dollar amounts.

The chart itself could display different colors that represent products sold in different months, and the legend would explain what each color represents.

By glancing at the column chart in Figure 11-3, you can quickly identify:

- ✔ Which products sell best
- ✔ How each product sells in each month
- ✔ Whether sales of a particular product are improving (or getting worse)

All this data came from the spreadsheet in Figure 11-3. By looking at the numbers in this spreadsheet, identifying the above information is nearly impossible. However, by converting these numbers into a chart, identifying this type of information is so simple even your boss could do it.

Although Figure 11-3 shows a column chart, Excel can create a variety of other types of charts so you can look at your data in different ways. Some other types of charts Excel can create include

- ✔ **Column chart:** Displays quantities as vertical columns that "grow" upward. Useful for creating charts that compare two items, such as sales per month or sales per salesperson.
- ✔ **Line chart:** Displays quantities as lines. Essentially shows the tops of a column chart.
- ✔ **Area chart:** Identical to a line chart except that it shades the area underneath each line.
- ✔ **Bar chart:** Essentially a column chart turned on its side where bars "grow" from left to right.

✔ **Pie chart:** Compares multiple items in relation to a whole, such as which product sales make up a percentage of a company's overall profits.

Excel can create both two- and three-dimensional charts. A 3-D chart can look neat, but sometimes the 3-D visual can obscure the true purpose of the chart, which is to simplify data and make it easy for you to understand in the first place.

Creating a Chart

Before you create a chart, you need to type in some numbers and identifying labels because Excel will use those labels to identify the parts of your chart. (You can always edit your chart later if you don't want Excel to display certain labels or numbers.)

To create a chart, follow these steps:

1. **Select the numbers and labels that you want to use to create a chart.**

2. **Click the Insert tab.**

   A list of chart type icons appears in the Charts group.

3. **Click a Chart icon, such as the Pie or Line icon.**

   The Create Chart gallery appears.

4. **Click a chart type.**

   Excel creates your chart and displays a Chart Tools tab.

Moving a chart on a worksheet

When you create a chart, Excel plops it right on your displayed spreadsheet, which may not be exactly where you want it to appear. Excel gives you the option of moving a chart to a different place on the current worksheet page or on a different worksheet page altogether.

To move a chart to a different location on the same worksheet, follow these steps:

1. **Move the mouse pointer over the border of the chart until the mouse pointer turns into a four-way pointing arrow.**

2. **Hold down the left mouse button and drag (move) the mouse.**

   The chart moves with the mouse.

3. **Move the chart where you want it to appear and release the left mouse button.**

Moving a chart to a new sheet

Rather than move a chart on the same sheet where it appears, you can also move the chart to another worksheet. That way your data can appear on one worksheet, and your chart can appear on another.

To move a chart to an entirely different sheet, follow these steps:

1. **Click the chart you want to move to another worksheet.**

   The Chart Tools tab appears.

2. **Click the Design tab.**

3. **Click the Move Chart icon in the Location group.**

   The Move Chart dialog box appears.

   As an alternative to Steps 1 through 3, you can right-click a chart; then when the pop-up menu appears, choose Move Chart.

4. **Select one of the following radio buttons:**

   • *New Sheet:* Creates a new worksheet and lets you name it

   • *Object In:* Lets you choose the name of an existing worksheet

5. **Click OK.**

   Excel moves your chart.

Resizing a chart

You can always resize any chart to make it bigger or smaller. To resize a chart, follow these steps:

1. **Move the mouse pointer over any corner of the chart until the mouse pointer turns into a two-way pointing arrow.**

2. **Hold down the left mouse button and drag (move) the mouse to shrink or expand your chart.**

3. **Release the left mouse button when you're happy with the new size of your chart.**

Deleting a Chart

Charts may be nice to look at, but eventually you may want to delete them. To delete a chart, follow these steps:

1. **Click the chart you want to delete.**

2. **Press Delete.**

You can also right-click a chart, then when the pop-up menu appears, choose Cut.

Chapter 12

Getting Organized with Outlook

· ·

In This Chapter

▶ Configuring e-mail settings and accounts

▶ Creating, reading, and replying to e-mail

▶ Adding and retrieving file attachments

▶ Deleting e-mail

▶ Working with names, addresses, and

▶ Utilizing appointments and tasks

· ·

*M*icrosoft Outlook is the personal organizer portion of Office 2010, able to handle information such as your appointments, names and addresses of important people, and list of to-do tasks. However, the most popular uses for Outlook are reading, writing, and organizing your e-mail.

Configuring E-Mail Settings

The first time you run Outlook, you need to configure your e-mail account information. To retrieve e-mail from your account within Outlook, you may need to know the following:

✔ Your name

✔ The username of your e-mail account, which might be JSmith (for Joe Smith)

✔ Your e-mail address (such as `JSmith@micro soft.com`)

✔ Your e-mail account password

✔ Your e-mail account type (such as POP3 or IMAP)

✔ Your incoming mail server name (such as `pop. microsoft.com`)

✔ Your outgoing mail server name (such as `smtp.microsoft.com`)

Outlook can often recognize many popular e-mail accounts such as Hotmail, but if Outlook can't set up your e-mail account automatically, you will need to ask your Internet service provider (ISP) for all these details.

Adding an E-Mail Account

Before you can use Outlook to manage your e-mail, you must add your e-mail account. To add a new e-mail account, follow these steps:

1. Load Outlook and click the File tab.

The Backstage View appears.

2. Click Info and then click the Add Account button.

An Add New Account dialog box appears, as shown in Figure 12-1.

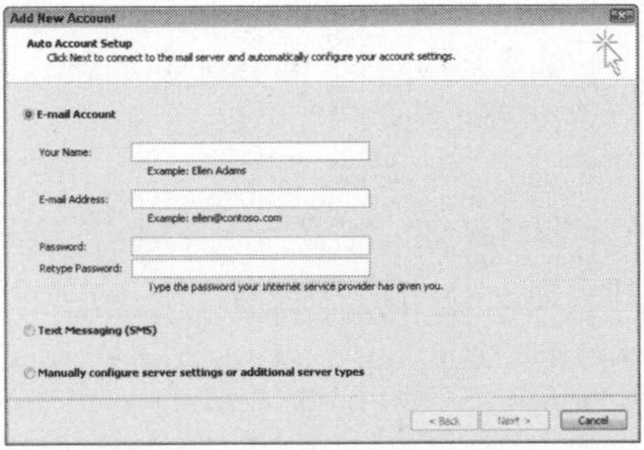

Figure 12-1: The Add New Account dialog box lets you create an e-mail account to work with Outlook.

3. Type in the appropriate information and click Next.

You may need to wade through several sets of questions before Outlook can properly configure your e-mail account.

To delete an e-mail account, right-click on the account name in the left panel of the Outlook window. When a pop-up menu appears, choose Remove.

Creating E-Mail

After you set up an e-mail account, you can start sending e-mail. The three ways to create and send e-mail are

- ✔ **Create a message and type the recipient's e-mail address manually.**
- ✔ **Reply to a previously received message.** Outlook then adds the recipient's e-mail address automatically.

✔ **Create a message and use a previously stored e-mail address.** Outlook adds the e-mail address automatically.

Creating a new e-mail message

The most straightforward way to send a message is to type the recipient's e-mail address and then type your message. To create a new e-mail message and type the e-mail address, follow these steps:

1. **Click Mail in the left pane of the Outlook window. (You can also press Ctrl+1.)**

   Outlook displays the Mail pane.

2. **Click the Home tab and click the New E-mail icon in the New category.**

   The message window appears. Notice that the message window displays a Ribbon with Message, Insert, Options, and Format Text tabs.

3. **Click in the To text box and type the e-mail address of the person you want to receive your message.**

   Make sure that you type the e-mail address correctly. One incorrect character, and your message won't go to your intended recipient.

4. **(Optional) Click in the Cc text box and type another e-mail address to send the message to more than one person.**

5. **Click in the Subject text box and type a brief description of your message.**

Many people use spam filters that examine the Subject line of a message, so it's a good idea not to type your subject text in ALL CAPITAL LETTERS or use multiple exclamation points!!! Otherwise, your recipient's spam filter may inadvertently flag your message as spam and delete it before anyone can even read it.

6. **Click in the message text box and type your message.**

   If you click the Save icon on the Quick Access toolbar, you can store the message in your Drafts folder so you can edit and send it at a later time.

7. **Click the Send icon to send your message.**

Replying to an e-mail message

Oftentimes, you may receive a message from someone else and want to send a reply to that person. When you send a reply, Outlook automatically copies the original message as part of your e-mail; that way, the recipient can read the original message that you're responding to.

Even better, when you reply to a message, you won't have to retype the recipient's e-mail address and risk misspelling it. To reply to an e-mail message, follow these steps:

1. **Click Mail in the left pane of the Outlook window. (You can also press Ctrl+1.)**

   Outlook displays the Mail pane.

2. **Click the Inbox folder.**

Outlook displays the Inbox pane that lists all the messages you've received.

3. **Click a message that you want to reply to.**

Outlook displays the contents of that message in a pane on the right side of the Outlook window.

4. **Click the Home tab and click the Reply icon in the Respond category.**

Outlook displays a message window with the recipient's e-mail address and subject line already typed in, along with a copy of the original message.

If you click the Forward icon instead of the Reply icon, you can send a message to another person instead of the person who originally sent you the message.

5. **Click in the message text box and type your message.**

If you click the Save icon on the Quick Access toolbar, you can store the message in your Drafts folder so you can edit and send it at a later time.

6. **Click the Send icon.**

Attaching Files to Messages

Rather than just send plain text, you can also *attach* a file to your message. This file can be anything from a picture, a song (stored as an audio file), a program, a video file, or even another e-mail message.

Be careful when attaching files to messages because many ISPs put a limit on the maximum size of an e-mail message, such as 10MB. Also try to keep any file attachments small because if the recipient has a slow Internet connection, downloading a large file attachment can take a really long time.

If you want to send someone a picture, video, audio file, compressed file, or even an entire program, you need to attach that file to a message by following these steps:

1. **Follow the steps in the earlier section, "Creating a new e-mail message," to create a new e-mail message, type a subject, and type an e-mail address.**

2. **Click the Insert tab.**

3. **Click the Attach File icon in the Include group.**

   The Insert File dialog box appears.

4. **Click the file you want to attach to your message and then click Insert.**

   Outlook displays an Attach text box in the message window.

   If you hold down the Ctrl or Shift key while clicking a file, you can select multiple files at once.

5. **(Optional) Click the Attach button to display the Insert File dialog box so you can select more files.**

6. **(Optional) Right-click any file in the Attachment text box; when a pop-up menu appears, choose Remove if you change your mind about attaching a file to a message.**

7. **Click the Send icon.**

Rather than select multiple files to attach to a message, you can compress or *zip* multiple files into a single compressed file by using a separate program like WinZip or by using the built-in Zip compression feature in Windows.

Retrieving a File Attachment from a Message

Rather than just send text, people might send you pictures, word processor documents, or databases as file attachments. When you receive a message with a file attachment, Outlook displays a paper clip icon next to the message.

Never open a file attachment unless you absolutely trust its contents. Many malicious hackers send viruses, worms, spyware, and Trojan Horses as file attachments, so if you aren't careful, you could accidentally infect your computer and lose your data.

To open a file attachment, follow these steps:

1. **Click a message that displays a paper clip icon.**

   Outlook displays the message's contents in the right pane of the Outlook window.

2. Double-click the file (paper clip) icon displayed in the message.

Your chosen files appear.

If you right-click on the paper clip icon in Step 2, a pop-up menu appears. Then you can click Preview and see a preview of the file contents without opening it.

Deleting E-Mail Messages

To keep your Inbox folder from getting too cluttered, you can always delete messages that you're sure you'll never need to read again. To delete a message, follow these steps:

1. Click Mail in the left pane of the Outlook window. (You can also press Ctrl+1.)

Outlook displays the Mail pane.

2. Click a message in the Mail pane that you want to delete.

3. Press Delete or click the Home tab and click the Delete icon in the Delete group.

If you accidentally delete the wrong e-mail message, you can undelete it by pressing Ctrl+Z or clicking the Undo icon in the Quick Access toolbar.

When you delete messages, Outlook stores them in the Deleted Items folder so you can always retrieve them later. To retrieve a deleted message, follow these steps:

1. **Click Mail in the left pane of the Outlook window. (You can also press Ctrl+1.)**

   Outlook displays the Mail pane.

2. **Click on the Deleted Items icon in the Mail Folders pane.**

   A list of deleted e-mail messages appears.

3. **Right-click on a deleted message and choose Move⇨Other Folder.**

   The Move Items dialog box appears.

4. **Click a folder (such as Inbox) to store your message and then click OK.**

   Outlook removes your message from the Deleted Items folder and stores it in the folder you chose.

If you delete a message from the Deleted Items folder, that message will be gone forever. To clean out your Deleted Items folder (to save space or to destroy incriminating e-mail messages), follow these steps:

1. **Click Mail in the left pane of the Outlook window. (You can also press Ctrl+1.)**

   Outlook displays the Mail pane.

2. **Choose one of the following:**

   - Click a message.

   - Hold down the Ctrl key and click each message you want to delete.

- Hold down the Shift key, click the first message you want to delete, and then click the last message you want to delete.

Outlook selects all the messages in between the first and last messages you selected.

3. **Press Delete or click the Home tab and click the Delete icon in the Delete group.**

A dialog box appears, asking whether you're sure that you want to delete your selected messages.

If you delete any messages from the Deleted Items folder, you will not be able to retrieve them ever again for the rest of eternity.

4. **Click Yes (or No).**

To help avoid unwanted e-mail messages, give out your e-mail address sparingly.

Storing Names and Addresses

Everyone has important names, addresses, e-mail addresses, and phone numbers that need to be saved. Rather than use Access or another complicated database program to store this type of information, it's much easier to use Outlook.

Adding a name

To store a name in Outlook, follow these steps:

1. **Click the Contacts button in the left pane of the Outlook window (or press Ctrl+3).**

   Outlook displays the Contacts view.

2. **Click the Home tab and click the New Contact icon in the New group.**

   Outlook displays a Contact window, as shown in Figure 12-2.

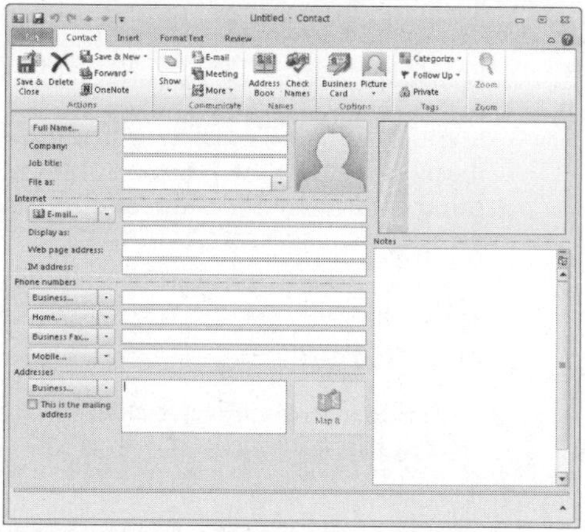

Figure 12-2: The Contact window lets you add data about a person.

3. **Type the information you want to store about each person, such as the name in the Full Name text box.**

   You can store as much or as little data about a person as you want. For example, you may not want to store someone's home phone number or IM (instant messaging) address.

4. **Click the Save & Close button.**

   Outlook saves your information.

Viewing names

After you've stored one or more names in Outlook, you'll probably need to find it again. If you just want to browse through your list of names, follow these steps:

1. **Click the Contacts button in the left pane of the Outlook window (or press Ctrl+3).**

   Outlook displays the Contacts view.

2. **Click the Home tab and click the Business Card or Card icon in the Current View group.**

   The Business Card displays names and additional information as large windows. The Card view displays names as smaller windows, allowing you to see more names on the screen.

   If you click on a name, you can delete it by clicking the Delete icon on the Home tab.

3. **Double-click on a name to open the Contact window.**

   The Contact window opens, allowing you to edit or add new information to your chosen contact.

Searching names

If you know all or part of a name or other information about a person, you can exhaustively browse through your entire list of stored contacts. However, it's much easier to just search for that information instead.

That way, if you know you want to find a person named Bill, you just have to search for "Bill." Likewise, if you know you need to call someone located in the 408 area code, you could just search for "408" and Outlook will show you all contacts with a phone number in that particular area code.

Searching makes it easier to find a particular name. To search for a name, follow these steps:

1. **Click the Contacts button in the left pane of the Outlook window (or press Ctrl+3).**

   Outlook displays the Contacts view.

2. **Click the Home tab and click in the Search Contacts text box (or press Ctrl+ E).**

   The cursor appears in the Search Contacts text box.

3. **Type as much data as you can about the person you want to find, such as typing all or part of a name or phone number.**

4. **Press Enter.**

   Outlook displays all contacts that match your search criteria that you typed in Step 3.

5. **Click the Close Search icon that appears at the far right of the Search Contacts text box.**

   Outlook displays all your contacts once more.

Setting Appointments

Everyone can get busy and miss deadlines and appointments. To avoid this problem, let Outlook keep track of your schedule. That way, you'll know what days and times you'll be busy and when you'll be free to do anything else.

Making an appointment

Before you can add an appointment to Outlook, you need to decide which day that appointment will occur and what time it will start. You can also add details like how long it should last and where it takes place, but the important part is to define the date and time. To do this, you need to look at the Outlook calendar.

Outlook offers several ways to display its calendar:

- ✔ **Day:** Displays a single time divided into 24 hours
- ✔ **Week:** Displays a single week divided into five or seven days
- ✔ **Month:** Displays a single month divided into days

Outlook lets you define starting and ending times of an appointment in half-hour increments such as 1:30 or 11:00 whether you're using the day, week, or month calendar. To set an appointment, follow these steps:

1. **Click the Calendar button in the left pane of the Outlook window (or press Ctrl+2).**

   Outlook displays the Calendar view.

2. **Click the Home tab and then click the Day, Work Week (5 days), Week (7 days), or Month icon in the Arrange category.**

Outlook displays the Calendar based on the time frame you chose, such as Work Week or Month, as shown in Figure 12-3.

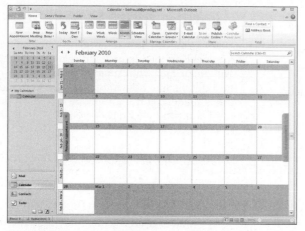

Figure 12-3: The month Calendar view in Outlook.

You can also click the New Appointment icon on the Home tab to define an appointment.

3. **Double-click the day (or time if you're in the Day calendar) where you want to schedule an appointment.**

   Outlook displays the Appointment window.

4. **Click in the Subject text box and type a brief description of your appointment, such as** Another boring meeting with Mike **or** Meet with reluctant client.

5. **(Optional) Click in the Location text box and type the location of your appointment, such as** Break Room 10 **or** Back alley near the dumpster.

If you often set appointments for specific locations, Outlook will remember these locations. In the future, just click the downward-pointing arrow in the Location text box and then click a previously used location in the list that appears.

6. **Click in the Start Time list box and choose a time.**

   You can also type a time directly in the Start time list box, such as 9:53, or even choose a different date.

7. **Click in the End Time list box and choose a time.**

   You can also type a time directly in the End time list box, such as 2:23, or even choose a different date.

8. **Click in the big text box and type any additional information you want to store about your appointment, such as items you need to bring or information you want to remind yourself about the person you're meeting.**

9. **Click the Save & Close icon in the Actions group.**

   Outlook displays your appointment in Day, Week, or Month view of the calendar.

If you need to edit an appointment, just double-click on it to display the Appointment window again. You can also drag an appointment from one location on the calendar to another to switch it to a different time or date.

Viewing appointments

If you store several appointments, you might find it hard to keep track of them all. To help you out, Outlook can display your appointments as a picture so you can see the times and dates when you have something planned.

To visually see your appointments, click the Home tab and then click the Schedule View icon in the Arrange group. Outlook displays your appointments so you can quickly spot your free and busy times, as shown in Figure 12-4.

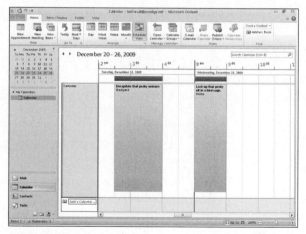

Figure 12-4: The Schedule View lets you see all appointments on a single day.

Deleting an appointment

After an appointment has passed or been canceled, you can delete it to make room for other appointments. To delete an appointment, follow these steps:

1. **Double-click on an appointment to open the Appointment window.**

2. **Click Delete (or press Ctrl+D).**

   Outlook deletes your appointment.

If you delete an appointment by mistake, press Ctrl+Z to recover it.

Managing Tasks

Everyone's busy. However, the big difference between busy, efficient people and overwhelmed people is that busy people simply know how to manage their tasks so they get things done.

Storing a task

A goal is simply a dream with a deadline. When storing tasks in Outlook, you need to define what it is that you want to do and set a date for when you want to complete it.

To store a task in Outlook, follow these steps:

1. **Click the Tasks button in the left pane of the Outlook window (or press Ctrl+4).**

   Outlook displays the Tasks view.

2. **Click the Home tab and click the New Tasks icon in the New group.**

   Outlook displays a Task window.

   If you just need to store a quick task, click in the Type a new task text box in the middle pane, type a brief description of your task, and press Enter.

3. **Click in the Subject text box and type a brief description of your task, such as** Sell tainted meat to my neighbor **or** Meet with police informant.

4. **(Optional) Click in the Start date list box and click on a date to start your task. Then click in the Due date list box and click on a date when you want to complete that task.**

   You don't have to add a start and end date, but it's a good idea to do so to help you measure your progress (or lack of progress) on your task.

5. **(Optional) Click in the Status list box and choose an option such as In Progress or Waiting on someone else.**

6. **(Optional) Click in the Priority list box and choose an option such as Low or High.**

7. **(Optional) Click in the % Complete box and click the up/down arrows to define what percentage you've completed of the task.**

8. **Click in the big text box to describe more details about your task.**

9. **Click the Save & Close icon.**

   Outlook displays your task.

If you double-click on a task, you can open the Tasks window so you can edit or add information to your chosen task.

Searching tasks

If you have a lot of tasks, you may want to find a particular one. To find a particular task, you can search for it. That way, if you know you want to find a task involving "Toxic chemicals," you could just search for "Toxic chemicals" and Outlook will display that task right away.

To search for a task, follow these steps:

1. **Click the Tasks button in the left pane of the Outlook window (or press Ctrl+4).**

   Outlook displays the Tasks view.

2. **Click the Home tab and click in the Search To-Do List text box (or press Ctrl+ E).**

   The cursor appears in the Search To-Do text box.

3. **Type as much data as you can about the task you want to find.**

4. **Press Enter.**

   Outlook displays all tasks that match your search criteria that you typed in Step 3.

5. **Click the Close Search icon that appears at the far right of the Search To-Do List text box.**

   Outlook displays all your tasks once more.

Chapter 13

Making Presentations with PowerPoint

• •

In This Chapter

▶ Creating a PowerPoint presentation

▶ Adding text

▶ Working with themes and backgrounds

▶ Adding graphics, movies, and sound

• •

*P*owerPoint works as a visual aid for giving presentations. (If you never give presentations, you probably don't need PowerPoint.) Instead of fumbling around creating, organizing, and displaying transparencies with an overhead projector, you can use PowerPoint on your computer to create, organize, and display slides that organize information as text and graphics.

Besides displaying slides on the screen, PowerPoint also lets you add notes and turn your entire slide show presentation into printed handouts so the audience can review your presentation with a printed copy of each slide. The next time you need to convince or inform an audience, use PowerPoint to create and deliver your presentation. (Just make sure that you never use PowerPoint to propose marriage, though.)

Creating a PowerPoint Presentation

A PowerPoint *presentation* consists of one or more slides where each slide can display text and graphics. Creating a presentation means adding slides and typing text or pasting graphics on each slide.

When you first start PowerPoint, the program loads a blank presentation that you can modify right away.

If you've been working on another presentation in PowerPoint and you need to start a new, blank presentation from scratch, follow these steps:

1. **Click the File tab.**

   The Backstage View appears.

2. **Click New.**

   PowerPoint displays different templates you can choose.

3. **Click Blank Presentation and then click Create.**

   PowerPoint displays a blank slide with a title and subtitle box, as shown in Figure 13-1.

After you create a new presentation, you need to fill it with *content* (text and graphics). PowerPoint gives you two ways to view, edit, and design your presentation:

- ✔ Slide view
- ✔ Outline view

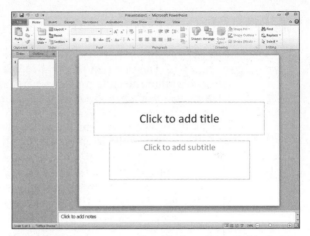

Figure 13-1: A new presentation consists of a single blank slide.

Both views let you add, delete, rearrange, and edit slides. The main difference is that *Slide view* lets you add graphics and modify the visual appearance of a slide. *Outline view* displays your entire presentation as an outline in which each slide appears as an outline heading, and additional text on each slide appears as a subheading. Outline view makes it easy to focus on the text of your presentation without the distraction of the visual appearance of your slides.

You can create an entire presentation in Slide view without ever using Outline view at all (or use Outline view without ever using Slide view at all). Outline view is most useful for creating and organizing a presentation. Slide view is most useful for viewing the appearance of multiple slides at once.

Working with Text

Most slides contain exactly one title and one subtitle text box. The title text box typically defines the
information that the slide presents, while the subtitle text box displays supporting information.

When you create a new slide, both the title and
subtitle text boxes will be empty, although they'll
both display the message `Click here to add
title` or `Click here to add subtitle`.
(This text won't appear on your slides if you don't
type anything there.)

If you delete all the text inside of a title or subtitle
text box, PowerPoint automatically displays the
`Click here to add title` or `Click here
to add subtitle` text in the empty text boxes.

To add text inside a title or subtitle text box, follow
these steps:

1. **Click in the title or subtitle text box, directly
   on the slide.**

   PowerPoint displays a cursor in your chosen
   text box.

2. **Type your text.**

You can also create title and subtitle text in Outline
view.

Typing text in a text box

A typical PowerPoint slide lets you type text in the
Title text box or the Subtitle text box. When you

type text in the Title or Subtitle text box, the contents appear as slide titles and subheadings within Outline view.

However, PowerPoint also offers you a third option for displaying text on a slide: You can create your own text box and place it anywhere on the slide.

To create and place a text box on a slide, follow these steps:

1. **Click the Insert tab.**
2. **Click the Text Box icon in the Text group.**

   The mouse pointer turns into a downward-pointing arrow.

3. **Move the mouse pointer over the area on the slide where you want to create a text box.**
4. **Hold down the left mouse button and drag (move) the mouse to draw a text box on a slide.**
5. **Release the left mouse button.**

   PowerPoint displays a text box.

6. **Type your text inside the text box.**

Any text you type into a text box that you create will not appear in Outline view.

Formatting text

After you create text in a text box, you can format it by choosing different fonts, font sizes, and colors. To change the appearance of text, follow these steps:

1. Click the Home tab.

2. Click in a text box and select the text you want to format.

3. Click one of the following font tools:

   - Font list box
   - Font Size list box
   - Increase Font Size
   - Decrease Font Size
   - Clear All Formatting
   - Bold
   - Italic
   - Underline
   - Shadow
   - Strikethrough
   - Character Spacing
   - Change Case
   - Font Color

Aligning text

PowerPoint can align text both horizontally and vertically inside a text box. To align text, follow these steps:

1. Click the Home tab.

2. Click in a text box and select the text you want to align.

3. **Click one of the following text alignment tools in the Paragraph group:**

   - Align Left

   - Center

   - Align Right

   - Justify

   - Align Text (Top, Middle, Bottom, Top Centered, Middle Centered, Bottom Centered)

4. **Click the Align Text icon in the Paragraph group.**

   A pop-up menu appears.

5. **Click a vertical alignment option, such as Top or Middle.**

Making numbered and bulleted lists

PowerPoint can display text as bulleted or numbered lists. The two ways to create such a list are before you type any text or after you've already typed some text.

To create a bulleted or numbered list as you type new text, follow these steps:

1. **Click in a text box.**

2. **Click the Home tab.**

3. **Click the Bullets or Numbering icon in the Paragraph group.**

   A pull-down menu appears.

4. **Click a bullet or numbering option.**

   PowerPoint displays a bullet or number.

5. Type any text and press Enter.

As soon as you press Enter, PowerPoint displays a new bullet or number.

If you have existing text, you can convert it to a bulleted or numbered list. To convert existing text into a list, follow these steps:

1. Click in the text box that contains the text you want to convert into a bulleted or numbered list.

2. Select the text you want to convert into a list.

3. Click the Home tab.

4. Click the Bullets or Numbering icon in the Paragraph group.

PowerPoint converts your text into a list.

PowerPoint displays each paragraph as a separate item in a bulleted or numbered list. A *paragraph* is any amount of text that ends with a paragraph mark (¶), which is an invisible character that you create when you press the Enter key.

Moving and resizing a text box

PowerPoint lets you move text boxes anywhere on the slide. To move a text box, follow these steps:

1. Move the mouse pointer over the edge of the text box that you want to move.

The mouse turns into a four-way pointing arrow.

2. **Hold down the left mouse button and drag (move) the mouse to move the text box.**

3. **Release the left mouse button when you're happy with the new location of the text box.**

To resize a text box, follow these steps:

1. **Click the text box you want to resize.**

   PowerPoint displays handles around your chosen text box, as shown in Figure 13-2.

Handle

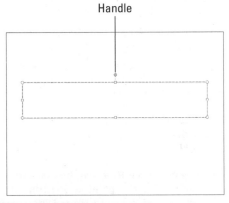

Figure 13-2: Handles let you resize a text box.

2. **Move the mouse pointer over a handle.**

   The mouse pointer turns into a two-way pointing arrow.

3. **Hold down the left mouse button and drag (move) the mouse.**

   PowerPoint resizes your text box in the direction you move the mouse.

4. **Release the left mouse button when you're happy with the size of the text box.**

Rotating a text box

After you type text in a title or subtitle text box, you can rotate the text box on your slide. To rotate a text box, follow these steps:

1. **Click the text box you want to rotate.**

   PowerPoint displays a rotate handle at the top of your text box.

2. **Move the mouse pointer over the rotate handle.**

   The mouse pointer turns into a circular arrow.

3. **Hold down the left mouse button and drag (move) the mouse to rotate your text box.**

   If you hold down the Shift key while dragging the mouse, you can rotate the text box in 15-degree increments.

4. **Release the left mouse button when you're happy with the rotated position of your text box (or press Esc to cancel the rotation).**

You can still edit and format text in a text box that appears rotated.

Applying a Theme

By default, PowerPoint displays each slide with a white background. Although you could change the colors and appearance of each slide individually, it's much easier to change every slide in your presentation by using a theme. A *theme* provides predesigned colors and designs that are applied to each slide to give your presentation a uniform and professional look.

To define a theme for a presentation, follow these steps:

1. **Click the Design tab.**

   If you click on a slide in the thumbnail view and hold down the Ctrl key, you can select which slides you'll change. If you don't select any slide, PowerPoint will change all your slides.

2. **Click the More button under the Themes group.**

   A menu appears.

   If you move the mouse pointer over a theme, PowerPoint shows how your presentation will look.

3. **Click a theme.**

   PowerPoint displays your chosen theme on your slides.

4. **Click the Theme Colors icon in the Themes group.**

   A menu appears, listing different color variations you can choose for your presentation.

5. **Click a color pattern.**

   PowerPoint displays your new theme colors.

6. **Click the Fonts icon in the Themes group.**

   A menu appears listing all the default fonts for your presentation.

7. **Click a font.**

8. **Click the Effects icon in the Themes group.**

   A menu appears listing all the different effects you can give your presentation, such as Metro or Clarity.

9. **Click an effect.**

Changing the Background

Another way to change the appearance of your presentation is to modify the background of your slides. PowerPoint provides predefined background themes that you can choose. To choose a background theme, follow these steps:

1. **Click the Design tab.**

   If you click on a slide in the thumbnail view and hold down the Ctrl key, you can select which slides you'll change. If you don't select any slide, PowerPoint will change all your slides.

2. **Click Background Styles under the Background group.**

   A menu displays different backgrounds you can choose.

3. **Click a background style.**

   PowerPoint applies your chosen background style to every slide in your presentation.

Adding Graphics to a Slide

Another way to spice up the appearance of your presentation is to include graphics on one or more slides. Such graphics can be informative, such as a chart that displays sales results; or they can be decorative, such as a cartoon smiley face that emphasizes the presentation's good news.

Three common types of graphics you can add to a PowerPoint slide include

- ✔ **Picture files:** Includes clip art images as well as images you may have stored on your hard drive, such as photographs from your digital camera
- ✔ **Charts:** Displays bar, column, line, pie, and other types of charts
- ✔ **WordArt:** Displays text as colorful text

Placing picture files on a slide

To liven up a presentation, you can add pictures you may have already stored on your computer. To add a picture to a slide, follow these steps:

1. **Click a slide (in either Slide or Outline view) to which you want to add a picture.**

2. **Click the Insert tab.**

3. **Click the Picture icon in the Images group.**

   The Insert Picture dialog box appears. You may need to change folders or drives to find the picture file you want.

4. **Choose the picture file you want and then click Open.**

   PowerPoint displays your chosen picture on the currently displayed slide. You may need to resize or move your picture.

Placing clip art on a slide

Clip art consists of drawings that come with PowerPoint. To add a clip art image to a slide, follow these steps:

1. **Click a slide (in either Slide or Outline view) to which you want to add a picture.**

2. **Click the Insert tab.**

3. **Click the Clip Art icon in the Images group.**

   The Clip Art pane appears on the right side of the screen.

   To access Microsoft's massive clip art library, you need an Internet connection.

4. **Click in the Search For text box and type a word that describes the type of image you want to find.**

5. **Click Go.**

   The Clip Art pane displays all the clip art images it could find that match the descriptive word you typed in Step 4.

6. **Choose the clip art image you want to use.**

   PowerPoint displays your chosen image on the current slide. (You may need to move or resize the image.)

7. **(Optional) Click the Close box of the Clip Art pane to make it go away.**

Resizing, moving, and deleting graphic images

When you add graphics to a slide, you may need to resize or move them to another location. To resize a graphic image, follow these steps:

1. **Click the graphic (picture, clip art, screenshot, or WordArt) that you want to resize.**

   PowerPoint displays handles around your chosen object.

2. **Move the mouse pointer over a handle.**

   The mouse pointer turns into a two-way pointing arrow.

3. **Hold down the left mouse button and drag (move) the mouse.**

   PowerPoint resizes your chosen graphic image.

4. **Release the left mouse button when you're happy with the new size of your graphic image.**

To move a graphic image, follow these steps:

1. **Move the mouse pointer over the edge of the graphic image you want to move.**

   The mouse turns into a four-way pointing arrow.

2. **Hold down the left mouse button and drag (move) the mouse.**

   PowerPoint moves your graphic image.

3. **Release the left mouse button when you're happy with the new position of your graphic image.**

After you add a graphic image to a slide, you may later decide to delete it. To delete a graphic image, follow these steps:

1. **Click the graphic image you want to delete.**

   PowerPoint displays handles around your chosen graphic image.

2. **Press Delete.**

   PowerPoint deletes your chosen graphic image.

Rotating graphics

You may want to rotate graphic images for added visual effects. To rotate images or to flip them vertically or horizontally, follow these steps:

1. **Click the graphic image you want to rotate.**

   PowerPoint displays handles around your image along with a green rotate handle.

2. **Move the mouse pointer over the rotate handle.**

   The mouse pointer turns into a circular arrow.

3. **Hold down the left mouse button and move (drag) the mouse.**

   PowerPoint rotates your graphic image.

   If you hold down the Shift key while dragging the mouse, you can rotate an image at 15-degree increments.

4. **Release the left mouse button when you're happy with the rotation of the image.**

Adding a Movie to a Slide

PowerPoint slides can also display a movie. When you store a movie on a slide, you can resize its size and move it anywhere on your slide. In case you need to modify it, PowerPoint will even let you trim parts of your video.

To add a movie to a slide, follow these steps:

1. **Click the slide (in either Slide or Outline view) to which you want to add a movie.**

2. **Click the Insert tab.**

3. **Click the top half of the Video icon in the Media group.**

   The Insert Video dialog box appears.

   If you click the downward-pointing arrow underneath the Video icon, a pull-down menu appears. Choose Video from File.

4. **Click the movie file you want to add and then click OK.**

   PowerPoint displays your video on the slide. If you click on the video, PowerPoint displays a Format tab underneath a Video Tools heading.

   If you click the Play button on the Format tab, you can view your video.

Adding Sound to a Slide

Sound can be as simple as a sound effect (like a gun firing to wake up people in the middle of your presentation) or a recorded speech from the CEO, explaining why everyone's going to be forced to take a 25 percent pay cut while the CEO gets a golden parachute of $500,000 a year for the rest of his life.

If you already have music, sound effects, or a speech stored as a file, such as an MP3 file, you can add it to your presentation. To add an audio file to a slide, follow these steps:

1. **Click the slide (in either Slide or Outline view) to which you want to add an audio file.**

2. **Click the Insert tab.**

3. **Click the top half of the Audio icon in the Media group.**

   An Insert Audio dialog box appears.

4. **Click the audio file you want to add and then click Insert.**

   PowerPoint adds your audio file to the currently displayed slide (represented as a horn icon). You may want to move the sound icon on your slide so it doesn't obscure part of your slide.

To hear your audio file, click on the audio file to display a Play button underneath. Then click the Play button.

Recording Audio

For greater flexibility, PowerPoint lets you record audio directly from your computer's microphone (if you have one, of course). Recorded audio lets you or someone else (such as the CEO) make comments that you can insert and play into your presentation.

To record audio for your presentation, follow these steps:

1. **Click the slide (in either Slide or Outline view) to which you want to add an audio file.**

2. **Click the Insert tab.**

3. **Click the bottom half of the Audio icon in the Media group.**

   A pull-down menu appears.

4. **Choose Record Audio.**

   A Record Sound dialog box appears.

5. **Click in the Name text box and type a description for your recording.**

6. **Click the Record button and start talking.**

7. **Click the Stop button and click OK.**

   PowerPoint displays your recording as a horn icon on the slide. You may want to move this horn icon to keep it from obscuring part of your slide.

The horn icon that represents an audio file won't appear when you show off your presentation.

Chapter 14

Storing Stuff in Access

• •

In This Chapter

▶ Understanding how databases work

▶ Creating a database

▶ Editing a database

▶ Viewing a database

▶ Searching, filtering, and sorting a database

▶ Closing a database

• •

A *database* is a program that stores information such as names, addresses, and phone numbers, or inventory part numbers, shipping dates, customer codes, and any other type of information that you think is worth saving.

To help you store information in a database, Office 2010 comes with the database program, *Access*. Access provides two huge advantages over storing information on paper. First, Access can store literally billions of chunks of information (try doing that with a filing cabinet). Second, Access makes it easy to search and sort through your information in the blink of an eye.

The three main advantages of a computer database over a paper database are

✔ **Massive storage:** The largest computer database can fit on a hard drive, but a paper database might take a roomful of file cabinets.

✔ **Fast retrieval:** Searching for a single name in a computer database is fast and easy. Doing the same thing in a paper database is difficult, error prone, and nearly impossible with a large database.

✔ **Reporting:** A *report* can help you make sense out of your data, such as showing a list of customers who earn a certain amount of money and live in a specific area. Trying to find this information in a paper database is time consuming and error prone.

Understanding the Basics of a Database

A database is nothing more than a file that contains useful information that you need to save and retrieve in the future. A database can consist of a single name and address, or several million names and addresses.

A typical Access database file consists of several parts:

✔ **Fields:** A *field* contains a single chunk of information, such as name, street address, or phone number.

✔ **Records:** A *record* consists of one or more fields. A business card is a paper version of a database record that stores fields (name, address, phone number, and so on) about a single person (record).

✔ **Tables:** A *table* displays records in rows and columns, much like a spreadsheet. Tables group related records, such as records of all your customers or records of all your invoices.

✔ **Forms:** A *form* displays all the fields of a single record on-screen, mimicking a paper form, so that you can add, edit, or view a single record at a time.

✔ **Queries:** A *query* lets you retrieve certain information based on your criteria, such as only retrieving names and addresses of people who earn more than $50,000 a year and have children.

✔ **Reports:** A *report* arranges your data in a certain way, such as showing all customers who placed more than 1,000 orders last year or all customers who live within a certain zip code.

Access is known as a *relational* database. Basically, this means that you can store data in separate tables and link or "relate" them together to avoid duplicating data in multiple tables. One table might contain customer names and addresses while a separate, related table might contain those same customers' purchase orders.

Here are the two basic steps to using a database. First, you need to design your database, which means deciding what type of information your database will hold, such as names, addresses, e-mail addresses, telephone numbers, and so on.

After you design a database, the second step is filling it with actual data, such as typing the name **Bob Jones** in the Name field or the e-mail address **BJones@somecompany.com** in the E-mail field.

When you first create a database, you'll probably start out with a single table that contains customer information. Inside the Customer Information table will be multiple records where each record represents a single customer. Each record will consist of multiple fields, such as Last Name, Company Name, Phone Number, and E-mail Address.

To help you edit and view your database table information, you might eventually want to create a form that displays your fields on the screen mimicking a paper form that's easy to read.

If you find yourself searching for the same type of information on a regular basis, such as looking for the names of your best customers (say, those who order more than $1,000 worth of products from you a week), you can store this search criteria as a query. Then you can just click on the query name and make Access show you exactly what you want to find.

Finally, you may want to print your data in a way that makes sense to you, such as printing a quarterly sales report. By saving your printing criteria in a report, you can make Access print selected data on a page that's easy for you to read and understand.

Features like forms, queries, and reports are optional but handy. Features like tables, records, and fields are necessary to store your information in your database.

Designing and Creating a Database

To design a database, you need to first create a database table and then define the names of all the fields you want to store in that particular table. Database tables let you divide a file into separate parts. For example, one database table may hold the names and addresses of all your customers, a second database table may hold the names and addresses of all your employees, and a third database table may hold the names and addresses of your suppliers. Access stores all this related information in a single Access file that's saved on your hard drive.

To design your database, you can create a database from scratch or use an existing template, which you can modify. *Designing* a database means defining both the number of fields to use for storing information and the maximum amount of data each field can hold.

If you have a field that stores numbers, what are the maximum and minimum limits on the numbers you want to save in that field? If you're storing someone's age, you probably don't want the field to contain negative numbers or numbers beyond 200. If your field needs to hold salaries, the field may need to hold large numbers but no negative numbers.

In general, store information in separate fields. So rather than create a single field to hold someone's full name, create two separate fields: One field holds a first name and the second field holds the last name. By storing last names in a separate field, you can easily yank last names out of your database to create form letters that state, "The <u>Smith</u> family has just won $200,000 dollars in the Publisher's Sales Pitch Sweepstakes!"

Access can create a blank database or a special database by using one of many templates available from the Microsoft Web site. No matter how you create a database, you will likely need to modify it to customize it for the type of data you want to store.

To create a database, follow these steps:

1. Click the File tab.

The Backstage View appears.

2. Choose New.

Access displays a variety of options, as shown in Figure 14-1.

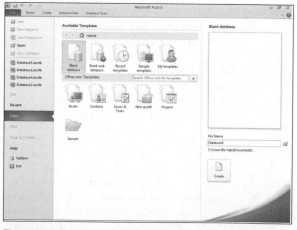

Figure 14-1: Creating a new database.

3. **Click on an icon such as Blank Database or a database template.**

   If you click on a template, the right pane shows a preview of your template.

4. **Click in the File Name text box and type a descriptive name for your database.**

   If you click on the folder icon that appears to the right of the File Name text box, you can open a dialog box that will let you define a specific drive and folder to store your database file.

5. **Click the Create button to create your database file.**

   Access displays your database.

Editing and Modifying a Database

After you create a database from scratch or from a template, you need to modify it by giving each field a descriptive name, defining the size of each field, or adding and deleting a field.

Naming a field

If you create a database from scratch, Access displays generic field names such as *Field1*. If you create a database from a template, you'll see the descriptive field names, but you may still want to rename the fields to something else.

To rename a field, follow these steps:

1. **In the All Tables pane on the left of the screen, double-click the table that contains the fields you want to rename.**

   Access displays the Datasheet view of your database.

2. **Double-click the field (column head) that you want to rename.**

   Access highlights the column.

3. **Type a new name for your field and then press Enter when you're done.**

Adding and deleting a field

Sometimes you may need to add a field to make room to store new information. Other times, you may want to delete a field that you don't really want after all. To add a field to a database table, follow these steps:

1. **Click on the downward-pointing arrow that appears to the right of the Click to Add heading.**

   A menu appears.

2. **Choose the type of field you want to add, such as Currency or Text.**

   Access inserts your field and gives it a generic name like Field3.

To delete a field from a database table, follow these steps:

1. **Click the field (column head) you want to delete.**

   Access highlights the entire column in your database table.

2. **Click the Delete button in the Add & Delete group.**

   If you have stored data in that field, a dialog box appears, asking whether you want to permanently delete all the data in the field.

   If you delete a field, you also delete any data that may be stored in that field. Depending on how much data you have stored, you could wipe out a lot of information by deleting a single field, so be careful.

3. **Click Yes (or No).**

   If you click Yes, Access deletes your chosen field.

Defining the type and size of a field

The *type* of a field defines the type of data the field can hold (numbers, text, dates, and so on), and the *size* of a field defines the amount of data the field can hold (no numbers larger than 250 digits, any text string fewer than 120 characters, and so on).

The purpose of defining the type and size of a field is to make sure that you store only valid data in a particular field. If a field is meant to store names, you don't want someone typing in a number. If a field is meant to store a person's age, you don't want the field to accept negative numbers.

To define the type and amount of a data a field can store, follow these steps:

1. **Click the Home tab.**

2. **In the All Tables pane on the left of the screen, double-click the table that contains the fields you want to define.**

   Access displays the Datasheet view of your table.

3. **Click the bottom half of the View icon (that displays a downward-pointing arrow), which appears in the Views group.**

   A pull-down menu appears.

4. **Click Design View.**

   Access displays the Design view of your database table.

5. **Click in the Field Name column and edit an existing field name.**

   If you click in a blank row, you can add a field to a database table.

6. **Click in the Data Type column.**

   A downward-pointing arrow appears.

7. **Click the downward-pointing arrow.**

   A pull-down menu appears, listing all the different types of data you can define to store in a field.

8. **Choose a data type, such as Number, Text, or Date/Time.**

   Access displays a General tab at the bottom of the screen, which contains different options for modifying your chosen data type.

9. **Click one of the data type options, such as Format or Input Mask, listed under the General tab.**

   Sometimes you have to type a value directly into a data type option. Other times a pull-down menu appears, from which you can choose an option.

10. **Repeat Step 9 for each data type option you want to modify.**

    You do not need to modify every data type option.

Using Datasheet View

Datasheet view is the default view for entering data. To view and enter data in Datasheet view, follow these steps:

1. **In the All Tables pane on the left of the screen, double-click a table.**

   Access displays the Datasheet view of your table.

2. **Click in a field defined by the column and row.**

   Each column defines a field, such as a name or address. Each row represents a single record.

   If you click in a field that already contains data, you can edit or delete that data.

3. **Press Tab to select the next field (or Shift+Tab to select the preceding field).**

4. **Type or edit the data in the field.**

Using Form View

The biggest problem with Datasheet view is that it can be confusing to find a field for a specific record. Because most people are familiar with paper forms or index cards that arrange related data (fields) on a page, Access offers you Form view.

Form view simply displays the fields of a single record on-screen. To use Form view, you must first create a form and arrange your fields on that form. After you create a form, you can add, edit, and view data through that form.

Searching a Database

A paper database is useful for storing information, but not so useful for finding it again. If you have a thousand business cards stored in a Rolodex file, how much time do you want to waste trying to find the phone number of a single person?

Searching a database is crucial to make your data useful, so Access provides two ways to search a database:

- ✔ Search for a specific record.
- ✔ Use a filter to show one or more records that meet a specific criterion.

Searching for a specific record

The simplest type of search looks for a specific record. To search for a record, you need to know the data stored in at least one of its fields, such as a phone number or e-mail address.

The more information you already know, the more likely Access will find the one record you want. If you search for all records that contain the first name *Bill,* Access could find dozens of records. If you just search for all records that contain the first name *Bill,* the last name *Johnson,* and a state address of *Alaska,* Access will likely find just the record you want.

To search for a specific record in a database table, follow these steps:

1. **In the All Tables pane on the left of the screen, double-click the name of the database table you want to search.**

   Access displays the Datasheet view of your database.

2. **Click the Home tab.**

3. **Click the Find icon in the Find group.**

   The Find and Replace dialog box appears.

4. **Click in the Find What text box and type in the data you know is stored in the record you want to find.**

   For example, if you want to find the phone number of a person but you know only that person's last name, you type that person's last name in the Find What text box.

5. **Click the Look In list box and choose Current field or Current document.**

6. **(Optional) Click in the Match list box and choose one of the following:**

    - *Any Part of Field:* The Find What text can appear in any part of a field.

    - *Whole Field:* The Find What text is the only text stored in a field.

    - *Start of Field:* The Find What text can be only at the beginning of a field.

7. **(Optional) Click in the Search list box and choose one of the following:**

    - *Up:* Searches from the record where the cursor appears, up to the beginning of the database table.

    - *Down:* Searches from the record where the cursor appears, down to the end of the database table.

    - *All:* Searches the entire database table.

8. **Click Find Next.**

    Access highlights the field where it finds the text you typed in Step 4.

9. **Repeat Step 8 to search for more records that might contain the text you typed in Step 4.**

10. **Click Cancel or the Close button.**

Filtering a database

Searching a database is easy but somewhat limited because you can retrieve only a record that matches any text that you want to find. If you want to find multiple records, you can use a filter.

A *filter* lets you tell Access to display only those records that meet certain criteria, such as all records that contain people who earn more than $200,000 a year, are currently married, live in Las Vegas, Nevada, and own two or more cats.

To filter a database table, you must tell Access which field to use as a filter, and then you must define the criteria for that filter. For example, if you want to filter your database table to see only those records listing the names of people who are at least 65, you filter the Age field and set the criterion to *Greater than or equal to 65.*

Filtering simply hides all records in a database table that don't match your criteria. Filtering doesn't delete or erase any records.

Sorting a Database

Sorting simply rearranges how Access displays your information. Sorting can be especially handy for rearranging your records alphabetically by last name, by state, or by country. You can also sort data numerically so that customers who buy the most from you appear at the top of your database table, while customers who don't buy as much appear near the bottom.

To sort a database table, follow these steps:

1. **In the All Tables pane on the left of the screen, double-click the name of the database table you want to sort.**

   Access displays the Datasheet view of your database.

2. Click the Home tab.

3. Click in a field (column) that you want to use for sorting.

4. Click the Ascending or Descending icon in the Sort & Filter group.

   Access sorts your records and displays an Ascending or Descending icon in the field name so you know you're looking at a sorted list.

5. Click the Remove Sorts icon in the Sort & Filter group when you don't want to view your sorted database table any more.

Querying a Database

One problem with sorting or filtering a database table is that you must constantly define what you want to sort or filter. In case you sort or filter your data a certain way on a regular basis, you can use a query instead.

A *query* is nothing more than a saved version of your sort or filter criteria. By saving the particular sort or filter criteria as a query, you can select that query by name later.

Creating a simple query

If your database table contains dozens of different fields, you may find it confusing to make sense of all your information. As an aid, a *simple query* strips away fields so you see only the fields containing data you want to see, such as a person's name and phone number but not her hire date or employee number.

To create a query, follow these steps:

1. **Click the Create tab.**

2. **Click the Query Wizard icon in the Macros &
   Code group.**

   The New Query dialog box appears.

3. **Click Simple Query Wizard and then
   click OK.**

   The Simple Query Wizard dialog box appears.

4. **Click a field name listed in the Available
   Fields box and then click the > button.**

   Access displays your chosen field in the
   Selected Fields box.

5. **Repeat Step 4 for each field you want to use
   in your query.**

6. **Click Next.**

   Another dialog box appears. This dialog box
   asks whether you want to display a Detail
   (shows every record) or Summary (shows
   numerical information such as the total
   number of records found, the average value,
   and the minimum/maximum value) view of
   your data.

7. **Select the Detail or Summary radio button
   and then click Next.**

   Another dialog box appears, asking you to type
   a descriptive name for your query.

8. **Click in the text box, type a descriptive name
   for your query, and then click Finish.**

   Access displays the results of your query as a
   separate tab.

9. **Click the File tab and then choose Save to save your query.**

Closing and Saving a Database

When you're done using a database file, you can either close it or exit Access altogether. Access gives you two options for closing a database:

- ✔ Close a single database table.
- ✔ Close the entire Access database file.

Part III
The Part of Tens

In this part...

No *For Dummies* book is complete without a Part of Tens section: chapters containing lists of ten easy-to-read informational nuggets. Of course, the lists don't always contain exactly ten, but you get the general idea.

The first Part of Tens chapter explains ten (or so) things you'll absolutely hate about Windows 7 (followed by ways to fix those problems).

Although Microsoft Office 2010 isn't something that you can pick up and figure out right away just by goofing around with it, you will find that Microsoft Office isn't necessarily as difficult to understand and use as you might have thought initially. In the second Part of Tens chapter, you discover various shortcuts and tips for getting the most out of Microsoft Office.

Chapter 15

Ten or So Things You'll Hate about Windows 7 (And How to Fix Them)

. . . .

In This Chapter

▶ Stopping the permission screens

▶ Finding the Windows 7 menus

▶ Turning off Aero Glass to speed up your PC

. . . .

*W*indows 7 certainly outshines its ungainly predecessor, Windows Vista. Still, you may find yourself thinking Windows 7 would be perfect if only . . . *(insert your pet peeve here)*. If you find yourself thinking (or saying) those words frequently, read this chapter. Here, you find not only a list of ten or so of the most aggravating things about Windows 7, but also ways you can fix them.

I Can't Stand Those Nagging Permission Screens

You can take either of two approaches to Windows 7's nagging permission screens:

- ✔ **Microsoft's preferred approach:** Before automatically clicking the Yes or Continue button, ask yourself this question: Did *I* initiate this action? If you deliberately asked your PC to do something, click Yes or Continue for the PC to carry out your command. But if the permission screen pops up unexpectedly, click Cancel, because something's wrong.

- ✔ **The easy way out:** Turn off the permission screens. Unfortunately, that leaves your PC more susceptible to viruses, worms, spyware, and other evil things tossed at your PC during the course of the day.

Neither option is perfect, but that's the choice that Microsoft has given you with Windows 7: Listen to your PC's occasional nags or turn off the nags and instead trust your own antivirus and antispyware programs.

I recommend Microsoft's preferred approach — it's much like wearing a seatbelt when driving: It's not as comfortable, but it's safer. Ultimately, though, the choice lies with your own balance between comfort and safety.

I Can't Copy Music to My iPod

You won't find the word *iPod* mentioned in the Windows 7 menus, help screens, or even in the Help areas of Microsoft's Web site. That's because Microsoft's competitor, Apple, makes the tremendously popular iPod. Microsoft's strategy is to ignore the little gizmo in the hope that it will go away.

What won't go away, though, are the problems you'll face if you ever try to copy songs onto an iPod with Media Player. You face two hurdles:

- ✔ Windows Media Player won't recognize your iPod, much less send it any songs or videos.

- ✔ When you plug in your iPod, Windows might recognize the slick gadget as a portable hard drive. It may even let you copy songs to it. But your iPod won't be able to find or play them.

The easiest solution is to download and install iTunes software from Apple's Web site (www.apple.com/itunes). Because iTunes and Media Player will bicker over which program can play your files, you'll probably end up choosing iTunes. (To settle the song-playing-rights battle, click the Start button, choose Default Programs, click iTunes in the Programs column, and choose Set This Program as Default.)

The Menus All Disappeared

In Microsoft's zeal for giving Windows 7 a clean look, the programmers swept away the folder menus used for the past decade. To reveal a folder's missing menus, press Alt. The menus appear, letting you choose the option you're after.

To keep the menus from disappearing again, click the Organize button, choose Layout, and choose Menu Bar from the pop-up menu.

The "Glass" Effects Slow Down My PC or Laptop

One of Windows 7's much touted special effects, Aero, may be too much for some PCs to handle. Aero makes your windows' frames translucent, letting bits and pieces of your desktop shine through them. The effects also let some programs, like Windows 7's chess game, "float" in the air, allowing you to watch the game from all angles.

But the calculations required for those visual gymnastics slow down PCs that don't have high-powered graphics — and that includes many of today's tiny laptops called *netbooks*.

Even worse, the fancy graphics may drain your batteries to a fraction of their battery life, and they can overheat your PC. If you don't like the extra burden Aero dumps on your PC, dump Aero by following these steps:

1. **Right-click a blank part of your desktop and choose Personalize to summon the Control Panel.**

2. **In the Basic and High Contrast Themes area, choose Windows 7 Basic.**

   That theme lives near the Personalization window's bottom. Your desktop's appearance changes as soon you select the theme's name.

If your computer is *still* too slow, try choosing Windows Classic in Step 2.

To turn Aero Glass back on for impressing your friends, follow the first step in the preceding list, but choose Windows 7 in the Aero Themes area.

If Windows 7 *still* isn't snappy enough, right-click Computer on the Start menu, choose Properties, and select Advanced System Settings from the task pane on the left. Click the Settings button in the Performance section, choose Adjust for Best Performance, and click OK.

My Quick Launch Toolbar Is Gone!

Many people didn't know what it was called, but the *Quick Launch toolbar* — that handy little strip of icons resting near the Start button — served as a single-click launching pad for favorite programs in both Windows XP and Vista.

Windows 7 strips the Quick Launch toolbar from its new, revamped taskbar. In the toolbar's place, the taskbar now shows three icons next to your Start button: Internet Explorer, Libraries, and Media Player. Don't like those icons? Right-click any offender and choose Unpin This Program from Taskbar from the pop-up menu.

You can also treat that portion of your taskbar as a makeshift Quick Launch toolbar by adding your own icons there. Follow these steps to copy icons from your Start menu to the taskbar:

1. **Click the Start menu and locate your cherished program.**

2. **Right-click the program's icon and choose Pin to Taskbar.**

   Feel free to rearrange icons on the taskbar by dragging them with the mouse to the right or left.

By pinning your favorite program's icons to the taskbar's *left* side, you can keep them separate from the taskbar's icons of *running* programs, which stay on the right side.

Windows Makes Me Log On All the Time

Windows offers two ways to return to life from its swirling and churning screen saver. Windows can return you to the opening screen, where you must log back on to your user account. Alternatively, Windows 7 can simply return you to the program you were using when the screen saver kicked in.

Some people prefer the security of the opening screen. If the screen saver kicks in when they're spending too much time at the water cooler, they're protected: Nobody can walk over and snoop through their e-mail.

Other people don't need that extra security, and they simply want to return to work quickly. Here's how to accommodate both camps:

If you don't *ever* want to see the opening screen, then use a single user account without a password. That defeats all the security offered by the user account system, but it's more convenient if you live alone.

1. **Right-click a blank part of your desktop and choose Personalize.**

2. **Click Screen Saver in the bottom-right corner.**

   Windows 7 shows the screen saver options, including whether or not Windows should wake up or resume at the logon screen.

3. **Depending on your preference, select or deselect the On Resume, Display Logon Screen check box.**

   If the check box *is selected,* Windows 7 is more secure. The screen saver wakes up at Windows 7's opening screen, and people must log on to their user accounts before using the computer. If the check box *isn't selected,* Windows 7 is more easygoing, waking up from the screen saver in the same place where you stopped working.

4. **Click OK to save your changes.**

The Taskbar Keeps Disappearing

The taskbar is a handy Windows 7 feature that usually squats along the bottom of your screen. Sometimes, unfortunately, it up and wanders off into the woods. Here are a few ways to track it down and bring it home.

If your taskbar suddenly clings to an edge of your desktop — or even the ceiling — try dragging it back in place: Instead of dragging an edge, drag the taskbar from its middle. As your mouse pointer reaches your desktop's bottom edge, the taskbar suddenly snaps back into place. Let go of the mouse, and you've recaptured it.

Follow these tips to prevent your taskbar from wandering:

- ✔ To keep the taskbar locked into place so that it won't float away, right-click a blank part of the taskbar and select Lock the Taskbar. Remember, though, that before you can make any future changes to the taskbar, you must first unlock it.

- ✔ If your taskbar drops from sight whenever the mouse pointer doesn't hover nearby, turn off the taskbar's Auto Hide feature: Right-click a blank part of the taskbar and choose Properties from the pop-up menu. When the Taskbar and Start Menu Properties dialog box appears, deselect the Auto-Hide the Taskbar check box. (Or, to turn on the Auto Hide feature, select the check box.)

I Can't Keep Track of Open Windows

You don't *have* to keep track of all those open windows. Windows 7 does it for you with a secret key combination: Hold the Alt key and press the Tab key, and a little bar appears, displaying the icons for all your open windows. Keep pressing Tab; when Windows highlights the icon of the window you're after, release the keys. The window pops up.

Or visit the taskbar, that long strip along the bottom of your screen. The taskbar lists the name of every open window. Click the name of the window you want, and that window hops to the top of the pile.

If a program icon on the taskbar contains several open windows — you're simultaneously editing several documents in Microsoft Word, for example — right-click the Microsoft Word icon. A pop-up menu appears, letting you click the document you want to access.

I Can't Line Up Two Windows on the Screen

With its arsenal of dragging-and-dropping tools, Windows 7 simplifies grabbing information from one window and copying it to another. You can drag an address from an address book and drop it atop a letter in your word processor, for example.

However, the hardest part of dragging and dropping comes when you're lining up two windows on the screen, side by side, for dragging. *That's* when you need to call in the taskbar. First, open the two windows and place them anywhere on the screen. Then shrink all the other windows into taskbar icons by clicking their Minimize buttons.

Now, right-click a blank area of the taskbar and then choose either Show Windows Stacked or Show Windows Side By Side. The two windows line up on the screen perfectly. Try both to see which meets your current needs.

Windows 7 introduces another way to align windows for easy dragging and dropping: Drag one window *violently* against a left or right edge; the window reforms itself to fill the screen's side. Quickly drag another window against the opposite edge, and they align themselves side by side.

It Won't Let Me Do Something Unless I'm an Administrator!

Windows 7 gets really picky about who gets to do what on your computer. The computer's owner gets the Administrator account. And the administrator usually gives everybody else a Standard account. What does that mean? Well, only the administrator can do the following things on the computer:

- ✔ Install programs and hardware.
- ✔ Create or change accounts for other people.
- ✔ Dial the Internet through a dial-up modem.
- ✔ Install some hardware, like some digital cameras and MP3 players.
- ✔ Perform actions affecting other people on the PC.

People with Standard accounts, by nature, are limited to fairly basic activities. They can do these things:

- ✔ Run previously installed programs.
- ✔ Change their account's picture and password.

Guest accounts are meant for the babysitter or visitors who don't permanently use the computer. If you have a broadband or other "always on" Internet account, guests can browse the Internet, run programs, or check their e-mail.

If Windows says only an administrator may do something on your PC, you have two choices: Find an administrator to type his or her password and authorize the action; or convince an administrator to upgrade your account to an Administrator account.

I Don't Know What Version of Windows I Have

Windows has been sold in more than a dozen flavors since its debut in November 1985. How can you tell what version is really installed on your computer?

Open the Start menu, right-click Computer, and choose Properties. Look in the Windows Edition section at the top to see which version of Windows 7 you own: Starter, Home Basic, Home Premium, Professional, Enterprise, or Ultimate.

In older versions of Windows, the version type appears on that same window, but beneath the word *System*.

My Print Screen Key Doesn't Work

Windows 7 takes over the Print Screen key (labeled PrtSc, PrtScr, or something even more supernatural on some keyboards). Instead of sending the stuff on the screen to the printer, the Print Screen key sends it to Windows 7's memory, where you can paste it into other windows.

If you hold the Alt key while pressing the Print Screen key, Windows 7 sends a picture of the current *window* — not the entire screen — to the Clipboard for pasting.

If you *really* want a printout of the screen, press the Print Screen button to send a picture of the screen to its memory. (It won't look like anything has happened.) Then click Start, choose All Programs, select Accessories, open Paint, and click the Paste icon from the top menu. When your image appears, choose Print from the main menu to send it to the printer.

I Can't Upgrade to Windows 7 from Windows XP!

The biggest delight enjoyed by Windows Vista owners could be sticking in an inexpensive Windows 7 Upgrade disc and transforming their PC into Windows 7: Their files and programs remain in place, and Windows Vista goes away forever.

Windows XP owners can also buy the upgrade disc. Unfortunately for them, upgrading to Windows 7 means wiping their hard drive clean and starting from scratch.

Chapter 16

Ten Keystroke Shortcuts

• •

*O*ne common theme of Office 2010 is that all programs look and work alike. After you learn how to use Word, you'll find it isn't much harder to learn Excel or PowerPoint because the Ribbon tabs all work in similar ways.

Even better, the same keystroke commands work alike in all Office 2010 programs. By memorizing the keystroke shortcuts in this chapter, you'll be able to work faster and more efficiently with Office 2010, no matter which particular program you may be using at the time.

Protecting Yourself with Undo (Ctrl+Z) and Redo (Ctrl+Y)

Many people are terrified of making a mistake, so they wind up never trying anything new that could save them time and make their lives easier. Fortunately, Office 2010 lets you freely experiment with different commands because if you do anything, such as delete or modify text or add a picture or page, you can immediately reverse what you just did by using the Undo command (Ctrl+Z) right away.

With the Undo command protecting you, you can try out different commands to see what they do. If things don't work the way you thought, press Ctrl+Z and undo your last changes.

If you wind up undoing a change and then suddenly realize you didn't want to undo that change after all, you can redo a command you previously reversed. To redo a command that you had undone, choose the Redo command (Ctrl+Y).

To undo multiple commands, follow these steps:

1. **Click the downward-pointing arrow to the right of the Undo icon on the Quick Access toolbar.**

   A pull-down menu appears of all the latest commands you've chosen.

2. **Highlight one or more commands on the Undo menu and click the last command you want to undo.**

3. **(Optional) If you undo a command and suddenly want to redo it, choose the Redo command by choosing one of the following:**

   - Click the Redo icon on the Quick Access toolbar.
   - Press Ctrl+Y.

Cut (Ctrl+X), Copy (Ctrl+C), and Paste (Ctrl+V)

Editing any file often means moving or copying data from one place to another. Understandably, three of the most common commands are the Cut, Copy, and Paste commands.

To use the Cut or Copy command, just select an item (text or picture) and choose the Cut or Copy icon on the Home tab (or press Ctrl+X to cut or Ctrl+C to copy).

Both the Cut and Copy commands are most often used with the Paste command. However, the Cut command, without the Paste command, is essentially equivalent to deleting selected text or objects.

Each time you choose the Cut or Copy command, Office 2010 stores that selected data (text or pictures) on the Office Clipboard, which can hold up to 24 items. After you cut or copy items to the Office Clipboard, you can always retrieve them.

If you turn off your computer or exit Office 2010, any items on the Office Clipboard are lost.

To retrieve a cut or copied item from the Office Clipboard and paste it into a document, follow these steps:

1. **Click the Home tab.**

2. **Click the Clipboard icon in the Clipboard group.**

3. **Move the cursor to where you want to paste an item.**

4. **Click an item displayed on the Office Clipboard.**

   Office 2010 pastes your chosen item in your file.

Saving a File (Ctrl+S)

Never trust that your computer, operating system, or Office 2010 will work when you need it. That's why you should save your file periodically while you're working: If you don't, and the power suddenly goes out, you'll lose all the changes you made to your file since the last time you saved it. If the last time you saved a file was 20 minutes ago, you'll lose all the changes you made in the past 20 minutes.

It's a good idea to save your file periodically, such as after you make a lot of changes to a file. To save a file, choose one of the following:

- Press Ctrl+S.
- Click the Save icon on the Quick Access toolbar.

The first time you save a file, Office 2010 asks you for a descriptive name. After you have saved a file at least once, you can choose the Save command, and Office 2010 will save your file without bothering you with a dialog box.

Printing a File (Ctrl+P)

Despite all the promises of a paperless office, more people are printing and using paper than ever before. As a result, one of the most common commands you'll use is the Print command.

To choose the Print command, press Ctrl+P or click the Print icon on the Quick Access toolbar.

Checking Your Spelling (F7)

Before you allow anyone to see your file, run a spell-check first. Just press F7, and Office 2010 diligently checks the spelling of your text. When the spell checker finds a suspicious word, it displays a dialog box that lets you choose a correct spelling, ignore the currently highlighted word, or store the highlighted word in the Office 2010 dictionary so it won't flag that word as misspelled again.

Spell checkers are handy and useful, but they can be fooled easily. You might spell a word correctly (such as *their*) but use that word incorrectly, such as *You knead two move over their*. Spell-checking won't always recognize grammatical errors, so you still need to proofread your file manually just to make sure that you don't have any misspelled or incorrect words in your file.

If you don't want Office 2010 to spell-check your entire file, just highlight the text you want to spell-check and then press F7.

Opening a File (Ctrl+O)

Generally, you'll spend more time working with existing files than creating new ones. Rather than force you to click the Office Button each time and find the Open command buried on the Backstage View, just press Ctrl+O instead. This immediately displays an Open dialog box so you can click the file you want to open.

Creating a New File (Ctrl+N)

Normally, if you want to create a new file in Office 2010, you have to click the Office Button and click New. Then you have to decide if you want to create a blank document or use a template.

Here's a quick way to create a blank document: Just press Ctrl+N. Office 2010 immediately creates a blank file without making you wade through the Backstage View.

Pressing Ctrl+N in Outlook 2010 creates a different item, such as creating a new e-mail message or task, depending on what you're doing with Outlook at the time.

Finding Text (Ctrl+F)

The Find command lets you search for a word or phrase buried somewhere within your file. To use the Find command, just press Ctrl+F. This opens a dialog box that lets you type the text you want to find.

Finding and Replacing Text (Ctrl+H)

Sometimes you may need to find and replace text with something else, such as replacing your cousin's name with your own name (especially useful for changing a will in a rich inheritance). To find and replace text, press Ctrl+H. When a dialog box appears, type in the text you want to find and the text you want to replace it.

When replacing text, you have a choice of using the Replace or the Replace All command. The Replace command lets you review each word before you replace it to make sure that's what you really want to do. The Replace All command replaces text without giving you a chance to see whether it's correct. When using the Replace All command, be aware that Office 2010 may replace words incorrectly. For example, in addition to replacing *Bob* with *Frank,* Office 2010 might also replace all occurrences of *Bobcat* with *Frankcat,* which is probably something you don't want to do.

Closing a Window (Ctrl+W)

To close a window, you can either click on that window's Close box or click the File tab and then click Close. For a faster alternative, just press Ctrl+W to close the current window right away.

If you haven't saved the contents of the current window, Office 2010 displays a dialog box asking if you want to save your data before it closes the window.

Index